THE ECLECTIC CURRICULUM IN AMERICAN MUSIC EDUCATION

CONTRIBUTIONS OF DALCROZE, KODÁLY, AND ORFF

EDITED BY POLLY CARDER

Revised edition

The National Association for Music Education

Copyright © 1972, 1990
Music Educators National Conference
1806 Robert Fulton Drive, Reston, Virginia 20191-4348
All rights reserved.
Published 1972. Second edition 1990
Printed in the United States of America
ISBN 0-940796-77-5

Contents

Preface to the Second Edition... v

Introduction 1

PART ONE
Emile Jaques-Dalcroze

The Dalcroze Approach
Beth Landis and Polly Carder 7

      Rhythmic Movement
      Original Exercises in Rhythmic Movement
      Solfège
      Improvisation
      Eurhythmics in Special Education
      Historical Development

The Timelessness of Jaques-Dalcroze's Approach
Arthur F. Becknell 31

The Importance of Rhythmic Training in Music Education
Annabelle S. Joseph 37

Eurhythmics, Aural Training, and Creative Thinking: The Dalcroze
Pedagogy for Children
Patricia Shehan Campbell 43

PART TWO
Zoltán Kodály

The Kodály Approach
Beth Landis and Polly Carder 55

      Sol-Fa Teaching
      The Instructional Repertoire
      Historical Development

Folk Song in Pedagogy
Zoltán Kodály 75

Zoltán Kodály's Legacy to Music Education
Egon Kraus 79

Folk Song in a Kodály-Based Curriculum
Sister Lorna Zemke 93

Can Kodály Help My Teaching?
Alexander Farkas 103

PART THREE
Carl Orff

The Orff Approach
Beth Landis and Polly Carder 109
  Speech
  Singing
  Movement
  Improvisation
  Instruments
  Historical Development

The *Schulwerk*—Its Origins and Aims
Carl Orff 137

What is the Orff-*Schulwerk* Approach to Teaching?
Konnie Saliba 145

Process and Improvisation in Orff-*Schulwerk*
Mary Shamrock 151

Carl Orff's *Music for Children*
Arnold Walter 157

References 161

Preface to the Second Edition

In music methods classes everywhere, future teachers are encouraged to study current trends and developments. They are expected to know what is new and to evaluate and compare instructional procedures and materials in what is and always has been an eclectic field. Perhaps more than any other teachers, those who teach music are expected to draw from available methods the ideas and materials that most nearly meet their students' needs. Even where curriculum guides are provided by the state or the local school system, the individual teacher is responsible for goal-oriented, day-to-day instructional planning, and for selecting and adapting appropriate materials and methods. Given the average class load and the usual restrictions on time, thorough preparation for teaching music classes is a serious concern.

The instructional approaches of Emile Jaques-Dalcroze, Zoltán Kodály, and Carl Orff have grown and prospered in the eclectic climate of American public school music. This is even more true today than it was eighteen years ago when the first edition of this book appeared. Some teachers choose to specialize in one of the three approaches. They receive certification at various levels from an expanding number of institutions or diplomas or degrees with concentration in a particular method. Other teachers take a more general view, however; they use the most typical techniques or materials of the Dalcroze, Kodály, or Orff approaches in a limited way. The teacher who uses sol-fa syllables is not necessarily teaching a Kodály program; using barred percussion instruments does not automatically mean that the Orff approach is being followed; and realizing music in movement does not constitute a Dalcroze program. American educators traditionally ask themselves what is being taught, and why. Continually reviewing *what* we teach and *why* is a valid way to make the best use of all instructional approaches, including those of Dalcroze, Kodály, and Orff.—*Polly Carder*

v

Introduction

American music education is and always has been highly eclectic. The strong style and content that can be recognized and identified as "American" has as its chief characteristic purposeful selection from available ideas. From Lowell Mason's course of musical instruction based on theories of Pestalozzi (who in turn had been influenced by Rousseau), to the present complex music curriculums in schools and universities, Americans have seen fit to adopt or adapt and develop any useful educational concept.

In recent years, three European musical doctrines have permeated practice in American schools: those of Emile Jaques-Dalcroze, Zoltán Kodály, and Carl Orff. The word *doctrines* seems inadequate to describe the ideas of these men, yet the ideas were not presented as fully sufficient and independent methods, even by their creators. American music education, at every age level, embraces vocal and instrumental performance, listening and analysis, experimentation, improvisation, and composition. It is based on literature that spreads from the latest in American popular music back through medieval plainsong, and from sounds of the Chinese *sho* to those of the synthesizer. In such a curriculum no one of the doctrines, nor all three together, can form a complete course of study. But as an approach, each doctrine, or adaptations of it, can contribute immeasurably to the complete or comprehensive American ideal.

The three doctrines are in some ways related, although each has its own purposes and practices. Both Kodály and Orff consciously learned from Dalcroze; Carl Orff said that he recognized the interrelationship of his instructional philosophy with that of Kodály; Kodály once visited the Orff Institute in Salzburg and purchased a set of the special instruments designed for the *Schulwerk*. Leaders of the Orff and Kodály movements visit each other in Europe and in the United States for interchange of ideas, and they successfully combine the two methods in workshops. All three men knew the usual plans of music teaching in their times, and discerning the weaknesses, tried to overcome them. Neither man created his system out of thin air. Each used the musical and educational principles he felt to be most useful in accomplishing his purposes and developing his own plan. Kodály adopted the hand signs that are basic to his plan of teaching note reading, after he observed music teaching in England and saw the signs being used in the Tonic Sol-Fa College founded by John Curwen. The chant and movement that are such useful and attractive components of Orff's teaching appeared first in the Dalcroze school.

The basic ideas on which successful teaching methods are built seldom are entirely new, nor do good ideas, as a rule, come to only one person. Change and progress in education often are based on ideas whose time has come. The fact that an idea has recurred again and again in educational practice indicates that it is worthy of our consideration. New and different approaches to persistent problems may result from creative application of an old idea. Furthermore, when musicians and thinkers of the stature of Emile Jaques-Dalcroze, Zoltán Kodály, and Carl Orff have developed systems they believe to be sound, educators naturally must take note of them.

One purpose of this book is to delineate as clearly and succinctly as possible the plan devised by each of the three musician-educators. The second purpose is to point out ways in which elements of the plans can be adapted to enrich and make more efficient the music teaching and learning in American schools. The individual teacher always has carried an important responsibility for awareness of current trends in educational thought, for making judgments of the values of these trends, and for putting into practice those procedures he believes best suited to his students. Referring again to Lowell Mason, whose work in public school music began in 1837, one might be surprised to read these statements from his *Elements of Vocal Music.*

> It is taken for granted in the following synopsis that the teacher is familiar with his work, or that he knows how to teach; pedagogic directions have therefore been mostly omitted; not even the questions common in such elementary works have been inserted, on the supposition that the man who is qualified to teach will *be able to ask his own questions.* The practical exercises, too, must be regarded as specimens; for as the good teacher of arithmetic does not rely exclusively upon his text book, but often gives out original or extemporaneous questions, growing out of the immediate circumstances by which he is surrounded, so the good music teacher will write lessons impromptu.... There is a freshness and lively interest in such lessons that cannot be reached by the most carefully prepared book exercises.... The best teacher will not be confined to any particular previously laid out plan, but will from the different methods make out one of his own; not indeed one that is stereotyped and unalterable, but

one that he may modify and adapt to the varying wants and circumstances of his different classes.[1]

It hardly seems necessary to rephrase Mason's statement for today's teacher. The need for awareness and application of all that can be known is greater than ever before. Modern pluralistic American society and the complexities of plans for school organization and grouping, coupled with the diverse innate natures and modes of learning of the individuals we teach, require, without doubt, every tool available to us.

Notes

1. Lowell Mason, *Manual of the Boston Academy of Music for Instruction in the Elements of Vocal Music on the System of Pestalozzi.* Boston: Boston Academy of Music, 1834.

PART ONE

Emile Jaques-Dalcroze

The Dalcroze Approach

by Beth Landis and Polly Carder

Emile Jaques-Dalcroze formulated his approach to music education earlier than Kodály or Orff, yet his instructional principles and procedures are particularly appropriate for today's music classes. During a long and varied teaching career that began in 1891, Jaques-Dalcroze met many of the same problems that confront music educators today. The teaching of music was divided into isolated compartments such as sight singing, form, and harmony without emphasis on the interdependence of these studies. Music students had, and still have, a clear need to develop the skills of musicianship, but Jaques-Dalcroze was frustrated by the fact that his students experienced difficulty in performing correct rhythms even though in ordinary physical movements they showed excellent rhythm.

Out of these and similar observations about shortcomings in his students' preparation grew one of the most unusual and influential methods in the history of music education, a method based on the idea that the source of musical rhythm is the natural locomotor rhythms of the human body. Today many people refer to the entire method as Eurhythmics, but the term used in that way is misleading. In a complete course of Dalcroze training, the studies that usually comprise a college music major's curriculum are included. Among them are singing, ear training, harmony, counterpoint, form, music history, applied music, and participation in vocal and instrumental ensembles.

Music instruction in the Dalcroze method involves three areas of study: solfège, aimed at developing an acute ear for sound; improvisation, for developing the capacity for free invention; and Eurhythmics, to give students a feeling for musical rhythm by means of bodily movement.

Eurhythmics, the only entirely new subject in the Dalcroze method, has always been associated with the name of Dalcroze, and is frequently considered as the sole area of study in his method. The areas of solfège and improvisation were incorporated by Dalcroze in his teaching of theory and harmony, however, before Eurhythmics was

7

developed and are considered of equal importance in Dalcroze training.[1]

Teachers today need to provide for the fullest awareness of self and for the fulfillment of each person's potential. The Dalcroze approach contributes to self-understanding by helping individuals to become aware of the expressive possibilities of their bodies and to develop those possibilities. In it, students recognize and develop the range of feeling inspired by music, sharpen their mental processes, coordinate them with physical and emotional processes, and cultivate a new expressive dimension that goes beyond the usual verbal one.

Self-development grows out of this awareness and understanding. In Dalcroze classes, the individual acquires skills that help in expressing the self fully and unselfconsciously. In a general philosophy such as that of the philosopher Abraham Maslow, self-actualization is described as the state in which a person performs toward the extent of his or her potential and is self-motivated and inner directed without need for extrinsic stimulus. Eurhythmics fulfills the goals implied in this definition, because it is an experience in which the person becomes absorbed in musical sound and the expressive possibilities of movement, and is led to perform beyond his or her own expectations. In this experience, the student learns to use the body as easily as the voice, and individuality is valued and encouraged. Dalcroze instruction assumes that the satisfaction that comes from a deep artistic experience has important effects upon a person.

Jaques-Dalcroze saw the weakness involved in a separation of musical studies. He planned for the development of a kind of musicianship that not only included accurate performance of the musical score but also called for a sensitive expression of all the interpretive elements of the music: dynamics, phrasing, nuance, and shading.

In the time of Jaques-Dalcroze and long afterward, education by principle without practice was common.

> When he asked his students to write down chords during their harmony classes he discovered that they were not really hearing what they had written, and that for most of them harmony was simply a matter of mathematics. It became clear to him that the traditional method of training musicians concentrated on the intellect to the detriment of the senses, and failed to give students a valid *experience* of the basic elements of music sufficiently early in their studies.
>
> He also noticed that although his students learnt to play their instruments and sing songs accurately, they did not think of their performance as a means of self-expression.... Technique had become an end in itself.[2]

Jaques-Dalcroze formulated his whole approach to music education on the synthesis of theoretical knowledge and skills and application of them. Sensory and intellectual experiences are fused. He believed that the skills and understandings of the least accomplished and the most accomplished musician alike are built on active involvement in musical experience.

The present-day emphasis on teaching musical concepts was anticipated by Jaques-Dalcroze. In his method, musical elements are encountered in numerous successive and concurrent experiences that lead to genuine understanding and skill. The element of rhythm is of first importance in early experiences. Changes in tempo and dynamics are heard and felt in the first lessons. Pitch, texture, and other elements are soon treated as a part of the sound palette. In ear training and dictation exercises, other elements are studied, and they are given further attention in improvisation exercises at the piano. Through movement, students can experience both the symmetry and the pull of the musical phrase. Qualities of rising and falling, greater and lesser intensity, and "towardness" can be effectively learned by students who are responding physically to music as they hear it.

Jaques-Dalcroze gave particular attention to the sequence of the student's musical training. He was especially concerned that instrumental study should not begin before ear training and rhythmic movement. He said, "I contend that an amateur should learn music before he touches the piano," and again, "It is veritable nonsense to have the child begin the study of instrumental music before he has manifested, either naturally or by training, some knowledge of rhythm and tone."[3] Contemporary writers in music education often have noted that a child's experiences with an instrument should be preceded by and concurrent with rich and varied experiences in listening, singing, dancing, and composing.

In the various organizational schemes of contemporary education, with new plans for grouping and scheduling and new demands for freedom and deep involvement, the Dalcroze approach to the study of music has much to offer. Groups of different numbers of students are not a detriment in this system—they may in fact be advantageous. Rhythmic movement lends itself to large and small groups, open spaces, and variable-length class periods. Tremendous impetus in rhythmic movement can come from large groups of students experiencing musical sounds together, according to authorities in Dalcroze work. Large and small spaces can be used advantageously. Activities in solfège and piano improvisation can be done in small groups. Some of the study of theory and harmony can be done through individualized instruction. Older and younger students can work together profitably and with pleasure. Through listening to music and experiencing it in movement, the children can develop healthy self-concepts, and their inner feelings can be explored, expressed, and shaped.

Observers are surprised to see how few textbooks are used by students of the Dalcroze system at all levels, from the smallest children to those preparing to teach the method. Of course, some of the areas of study, such as music history and literature, are largely dependent on textbook materials; but a great many principles of music theory, form, and vocal technique are learned through participation. Exercises are often notated on chalkboards by the teacher or the students according to the purpose of the exercise. Furthermore, Jaques-Dalcroze said that teachers cannot learn his system of musical instruction from books and musical scores—that participation in training classes is the only effective way of learning the subject. The stress on the feelings of the student in response to music (and on the channeling of these feelings into expression) is important to the Dalcroze plan. Dalcroze teachers think personal experience is the only way of learning this system. The ideas must be tried to be evaluated. Individuality is stressed, and the teacher who adopts ideas from the method must trust his or her own individuality and find ways to apply the principles to the practice of teaching in his or her own way. One qualification of the teacher about which Jaques-Dalcroze had a great deal to say is ability to improvise at the piano.

> The reader must remember that all the music is improvised. From the very nature of the exercises it is impossible to use written music. M. Jaques-Dalcroze has composed, in addition to his *Action Songs* for children, music which may be used in plastic exercises and these are occasionally employed by the teacher; but for the most part the music must be created spontaneously. That is why the method in its complete form lays so much stress on ear-training and improvisation; and that is

10

also why those who profess to be Dalcroze teachers after a few lessons in rhythmic movement can only offer the husk of this training. The whole kernel is lacking—the understanding of musical harmony, the ability to improvise rhythms illustrative of the various musical principles and laws, and worst lack of all the ability to improvise exercises by combining the elements of several already given.[4]

The teacher's ability to improvise at the piano is absolutely essential if the method is to be used as Jaques-Dalcroze intended. This includes the ability to create a different "movement feeling" for each exercise since students learn to let music move them in whole-body responses. The music that is played must be completely appropriate to the idea being taught, whether that idea is crescendo, or largo, or the rise and fall of a melodic phrase.

Rhythmic Movement

Although the Dalcroze method consists of three main branches, Eurhythmics (rhythmic movement), solfège, and piano improvisation, the approach is based on the experience of rhythm through body movement—and this experience dominates the early lessons. Jaques-Dalcroze first used rhythmic movement as a mode of instruction in solfège classes and in private lessons. Today in Dalcroze training, Eurhythmics is used in all classes to teach practically every aspect of music. Jaques-Dalcroze believed that rhythm is the fundamental, motivating force in all the arts, especially in music. He recognized that human life is characterized by rhythms such as those of the heartbeat and of breathing. He based his teaching on the principle that musical rhythms parallel the rhythms of life. In music, rhythm is actually motion: the animating factor that gives continuity and impetus to sounds. In the Dalcroze technique, all types of motion found in music are studied through rhythmic movement. Even exercises in solfège and improvisation are introduced through rhythm and are done in rhythm. Standard classroom percussion instruments, such as sticks, triangles, tambourines, sand blocks, and small drums are used extensively in classes for adults as well as children. Their function is to extend the possibilities of muscular responses to music.

Of the three elements he found in music—sound, rhythm, and dynamics, the last two depended entirely on movement and had their counterpart in our muscular systems. Changes of tempo (allegro, andante, etc.) and dynamics (forte, piano, crescendo, diminuendo) could be expressed by our bodies, and the intensity of our musical feelings depended on the intensity of our physical sensations.[5]

11

With rhythmic movement as the basic mode of instruction, musical concepts are internalized. Jaques-Dalcroze planned to teach the elements—rhythm, melody, harmony, dynamics, form, and phrasing—through leading his students to experience these things in movement. He believed that immediate physical response—realizing the music as it is heard—is essential to the comprehension of a musical idea. Rhythmic movement is the means by which all the different kinds of movement in music, such as the flow of melody, the shifting of harmony, the phrase that can be analogous with a human breath, can be known. In the words of Jaques-Dalcroze:

> It is my object, after endeavoring to train the pupil's ear, to awaken in him, by means of special gymnastics, the sense of his personal body-rhythm, and to induce him to give metrical order to the spontaneous manifestations of his physical nature. Sound rhythms had to be stepped, or obtained by gestures; it was also necessary to find a system of notation capable of measuring the slightest nuances of duration, so as to respond to both the demands of the music and to the bodily needs of the individual.[6]

In his writings, Jaques-Dalcroze used the term "sound" to mean a combination of pitch, timbre, and dynamics. He seemed to include in this term all aspects of musical tone except rhythm. The word "gymnastics" he used to mean rhythmic movement. He found it an unsatisfactory term when he first used it, and certainly today it does not convey the essential meaning of the method. The word "rhythm" he used to mean movement in music. In its narrow sense, this means the *takt* or measure beat and the subdivisions of that beat. In his usage, however, it includes the concepts of melodic rhythm, harmonic rhythm, word rhythms in vocal music, and the rhythm patterns of accompaniment figures. In an even wider sense it includes dynamic intensity, the balance of equal and unequal phrases, and elements of the formal structure of a composition that give it drive, impetus, or motion. Students of the Dalcroze method are taught that rhythm is really motion, and they become aware of all the ways in which motion is evident in music.

In typical Dalcroze classes, a musical concept such as that of accelerando is built gradually. It may begin with an imaginative idea such as the representation of a person or object in the act of gaining speed. This movement is done first without music; it should be a familiar movement from daily life. Then the student listens to music in which accelerando is unmistakable, and discovers movement that corresponds with what he or she has just done. This prepares the student to synchronize his or her movement spontaneously with appropriate music. Recognition of the term "accelerando" follows.

12

Other musical concepts are built in the same way. In a later lesson, the student sees the written symbol for accelerando, responds with muscular sensations, and uses the idea in notation and in improvisation. A basic principle of this method is that time, space, and energy are interrelated. By synchronizing their movements with music as they hear it, students experience these interrelationships. They analyze simultaneous elements and successive musical events by realizing them in movement. For example, by walking on tiptoe, with steps becoming longer and longer, stretching forward and upward while bringing more of the foot down with each successive step, making larger and larger movements, students "realize" a crescendo.

In Eurythmics classes, students move freely with music improvised by the teacher at the piano. In bare feet and comfortable clothing, class members skip, walk, run, and leap through movements that are evoked by the musical sounds. Intrinsic to the process is intensive listening—listening that is natural because the physical response depends on it. The spontaneous quality of the movement is derived from the fact that the music is being created while students listen. The music will be different for each successive exercise, and responses cannot be anticipated.

> A striking phenomenon in lessons in Eurhythmics is the extreme diversity of individual movements on the part of those who do the same exercises together, to the same music. In other words, there are great differences of interpretation of the same musical rhythms by different persons. This variety corresponds exactly to the personal characteristics of the various pupils, and it may be interesting to see why this individual factor, so striking in our classes, is absent in gymnastic or military exercises where hundreds of individuals do the same movement in the same way. The reason is that the gestures of pupils are the manifestation of their higher will imposing certain rhythms on their bodily movements. Exercises in athletics or drill aim at a purely material object, whereas we endeavor to produce a common outward expression of individual emotions. Here rhythm is the link between mind and senses, and this to such a degree that each pupil speedily rejects the current opinion which looks upon the body as inferior to the mind. He quickly comes to regard his body as an instrument of incomparable delicacy, susceptible of the noblest and the most artistic expression.[7]

Each student has natural characteristic movements and styles of moving that give a unique quality to his or her work. Jaques-Dalcroze recognized this fact and capitalized on it. Each student feels the music in the deepest sense and expresses it unselfconsciously with the entire body. Jaques-Dalcroze believed that when this idea is carried to its logical extreme, the

13

body will become a musical instrument. The student will hear, analyze, internalize, and become one with the music.

The basic rhythms played at the piano by the teacher match natural rhythms of human movement, such as walking, running, skipping, and swinging. A teacher often asks a student to begin a specific movement and, watching the tempo and intensity of the response, plays in that tempo and at that dynamic level. There is a natural development from simple basic movements to complex movements, in which students may interpret a canon or several musical elements simultaneously. As a musical instrument, the body is called upon to perform in complex ways, often with the arms interpreting one pattern, the feet another, and other parts of the body others. For example, the arms may conduct in ¼ meter while the feet move with a syncopated rhythmic pattern and the head nods on specified beats. In another exercise, the teacher plays one measure before the students begin to move. The students then respond to the first measure as they listen to the second (and so on through the composition).

In a different exercise, students speak or sing one pattern or rhythm with a text and perform a different pattern in movement. Students learn to expect sudden change in the music and to respond at once. The change may be in tempo, dynamics, or meter. For example, the change may consist of a contrasting style of music, or of small variations on a single element. Students respond instantly and in good form to what they hear. A result of such exercises is the ability to respond sensitively to the most refined nuances in music. Students express the controlled arching of phrases and intricate shadings of timbre, tempo, and dynamics, in addition to basic musical elements. This is what Jaques-Dalcroze meant when he spoke of the body as a musical instrument. An observer has the interesting experience of seeing people feel music: a teacher, watching students respond to music in this way, is concerned entirely with movement as evidence of the students' comprehension of musical elements. The students are not performing for others; they are internalizing musical concepts through physical experience.

In Europe in the late nineteenth century, at the time Jaques-Dalcroze conceived of rhythmic movement as a form of music education, there was a growing interest in gymnastics and in new forms of dance. A freer kind of interpretive dance was developing in opposition to the stereotyped, mannered style of the classical ballet. In this new form called modern dance, the Americans Isadora Duncan, Ted Shawn, and Ruth St. Denis became leaders. Jaques-Dalcroze insisted that he was not a teacher of the dance, and that all his innovations in rhythmic movement were made for the sole purpose of teaching music, but some people consider that he made a great contribution to the art of the dance. He greatly increased the possibilities of gesture by having people experiment with space, moving different parts of their bodies in different spatial planes. The call for intense concentration on listening to music and the correlation of movement with music were naturally beneficial to dancers.

Mary Wigman studied with Jaques-Dalcroze for several years and then, using some of the principles he taught, built a most successful career as a dancer. Ted Shawn and Ruth St. Denis directed that the members of their troupe, the Denishawn Dancers, study the Dalcroze work; Martha Graham and Doris Humphries were in this group. Among others who explored the possibilities of Jaques-Dalcroze's principles for choreography were Vaslav Nijinsky and George Balanchine.

Leading teachers of the Dalcroze method today, however, reiterate the statement of the originator: "We are teaching music, not the dance." While he was teaching a solfège class, about 1895, Jaques-Dalcroze observed some inadequacies in the singing. At this time, he devised exercises to be done in a sitting position, with arms and hands alone, to improve the feeling for melodic line. In 1902 he directed that whole-body movements be done. He also insisted that students have bare feet—a practice that was absolutely shocking at the time.

Original Exercises in Rhythmic Movement

After he had taught for a while using the plan of developing musical skills and understandings through rhythmic movement, Jaques-Dalcroze made a written record of some of the exercises he had devised. Today these exercises, translated into English, give much less than a complete insight into the procedures used in Eurhythmics classes. Jaques-Dalcroze realized that the spontaneity essential to his method would be lost in writing about it. He explained that the exercises he wrote were meant for those who had studied in his classes as reminders of some of their most productive learning experiences. Sixty-six exercises were described in *Rhythm, Music and Education* (twenty-two under the heading of "Rhythmic Movement" and the same number under each of the headings "Solfege or Aural Training" and "Pianoforte Improvisation"). Ten representative exercises are quoted here from an adaptation of Jaques-Dalcroze's book *The Importance of Being Rhythmic: A Study of the Principles of Dalcroze Eurhythmics Applied to General Education and to the Arts of Music, Dancing, and Acting* by Jo Pennington. They give some idea of the way in which instructional procedures in Eurhythmics were described during the years when they first became known in the United States.

Exercises in Rhythmic Movement

In order that the reader may have some definite idea of the nature of the exercises in rhythmic movement, we shall describe those listed in the following program. This program is selected because it was given at a public demonstration lesson of eurythmics and because it gives representative exercises. These exercises are merely a sample—just such an introduction to an understanding of the Dalcroze method as an understanding of the alphabet is an introduction to the English language. They are described here merely to give a definite focus to the general principles set forth in the early part of this chapter; to show how those principles have been framed in the form of exercises.

Exercise 1. Following the Music, Expressing Tempo and Tone Quality

The teacher at the piano improvises music to which the pupils march (usually in a circle) beating the time with their arms ($\frac{3}{4}$, $\frac{5}{8}$, $\frac{12}{8}$, etc.) as an orchestra leader conducts, and stepping with their feet the note values (that is, quarter notes are indicated by normal steps, eighth notes by running steps, half notes by a step and a bend of the leg, a dotted eighth and a sixteenth by a skip, etc.). The teacher varies the expression of the playing, now increasing or decreasing the intensity of tone, now playing more slowly or more quickly; and the pupils "follow the music" literally, reproducing in their movements the exact pattern and structure of her improvisation.

Exercise 2. Attention and Inhibition

These two exercises of attention and inhibition are exercises in mental control, concentration and coordination of mind and body. In (a) the pupils march to the music and at "hopp" take one step backward. As this word comes at quite irregular intervals and they have no warning of it, they must listen carefully and be ready to respond, both

16

mentally and muscularly, the moment they hear the command. In (b) the pupils march to the music and at a signal stop and count silently the two, three, four or more beats agreed upon and then take up their march exactly on time. This is an exercise in silent counting, demanding concentration and a consciousness of the beat in the muscles as well as in the brain—a kind of training in muscular memory. It is amusing to note how unfailingly beginners take up the marching too soon, seldom too late. The tendency of the untrained mind is to quicken the beat while the music is silent because the mind operates consciously whereas the muscles should record and retain the impression without conscious effort.

Exercise 3. Arm Movements to Indicate Measure

As explained in the first exercise, the movements of the arm indicate the measure of the music. They are modeled on those of the orchestra conductor. In two-four time the arms move down for the metric accent and then up for the second beat; in three-four they move down, sideways and then up; in four-four, they move down, crossed in front of the body, sideways and then up, etc.

Exercise 4. Note Values. Syncopation

In the exercise to demonstrate note values, the pupils march one step for each beat while the teacher plays quarter notes; two for each beat in eighth notes; three for triplets, etc. The values of whole and half notes are also represented, the half note by a step and a bend, and the whole note by a step followed by three or more movements of the leg without stepping. Exercises in syncopation require more training. The teacher plays an even tempo—say quarter notes in four-four time. The pupils at a command walk in syncopation for one measure or more—stepping either just before or just after the beat...anticipating the beat or retarding it. As their *feet* take steps just *off the beat*, their *arms* must continue to beat the time regularly, each movement being made *on the beat*. This exercise then is one in concentration, mental and physical control (coordination) and in the understanding of the musical principles of polyrhythm and syncopation.

Exercise 5. Conducting

In the exercise in conducting, one pupil takes his place before the others and conducts them just as the leader of an orchestra conducts, indicating the tempo the pupils are to take in their marching, directing crescendo and diminuendo at will, quicker and slower speeds, heaviness or lightness of feeling to be expressed in their movements, accents to be made, (other than the metric accent on the first beat of each measure which is always indicated by a stamp of the foot). These accents on beats other than the first are pathetic accents. This exercise is first of all an exercise in self-control and spontaneous improvisation in rhythmic movement on the part of the "conductor"; on the part of the pupils it is the same as the first exercise of this program.

Exercise 6. Phrasing

Everyone knows that music, like speech, is broken up into phrases. A singer pauses to take a fresh breath at the beginning of a new phrase. In movement a new phrase may be indicated in several ways: such as a change of direction of the march on the part of the whole group, or by a change from one arm to another on the part of the individual. This is an exercise in ear-training, in attention and in the creation of new ways of expressing the beginning of a phrase, that is, improvisation.

Exercise 7. "Realization" of Rhythms

As explained in the program, to "realize" in the Dalcroze sense means to express in bodily movements all the elements of the music save sound. In this exercise the teacher plays a series of measures and the pupils, after listening to them, realize in their movements the rhythm which they have heard—expressing the note values, the meter, the shading, the quickness or slowness—they reproduce the rhythm in movement as definitely as though it were written in ordinary musical notation. In fact that is usually the next step in the exercise. This exercise combines several important elements of Dalcroze Eurythmics: ear training; the musical analysis of rhythm; memory and concentration; and the physical response necessary to the execution of the rhythm in movement.

Exercise 8. Exercise in Canon

The teacher improvises measures in a given meter and the pupils realize the rhythm of each measure just after its execution by the teacher; that is, in canon. This exercise combines the principles of exercises 1, 2, 3, 4 and 7 and adds to it the close concentration required to listen to one measure while executing the preceding one. Everyone knows those old songs, "Scotland's Burning" and "Three Blind Mice" in which one singer begins and sings one phrase; the second singer begins later and so on. This exercise follows the same musical principle. No pupil of eurythmics will ever quail before the legendary terrors of a "Bach Fugue" who has arrived at an understanding of the principle of canon for that is the basis of the composition of a fugue.

Exercise 9. Independence of Control

This exercise is one in polyrhythm, the pupil expressing several rhythms at the same time. He may perhaps beat three-four time with the left arm and four-four with the right at the same time walking twelve-eight with the feet. There are many variations of this though in the beginning pupils find it sufficiently difficult to beat two with one arm and three with the other, especially since each arm must "remember" so to speak, the accent which falls on the first beat of its own measure. Another form of this exercise is to have the pupils march one measure while beating time for another; as three with the arms and four with the feet. These are worked out mathematically at first but soon the pupils learn to keep in their muscular and mental consciousnesses the pulse of the two rhythms simultaneously.

Exercise 10. Rhythmic Counterpoint

Rhythmic counterpoint[8] is an exercise in the appreciation of unplayed beats. The teacher improvises a short theme, let us say simply two half notes and a quarter in five-four time. The pupil, instead of stepping on the first, third and fifth beats of the measure, will do the counterpoint by stepping on the *second and fourth*. Or, if told to do the counterpoint in eighth notes, he will fill in every unplayed eighth note beat. This is an exercise in inhibition and in the accurate analysis of time values.

A more complicated form of exercise is the realization of theme and counterpoint simultaneously. For example, the pupils may learn a simple melody for a theme and then proceed to sing this melody while executing a rhythmic counterpoint, as a sort of accompaniment, with steps, or with gestures. This is a very interesting exercise to watch for first one hears the note played by the teacher and following it the steps taken by the pupils to fill in the measure, the whole making a sound pattern as well as a rhythmic pattern.[9]

Solfège

Dalcroze believed that the study of Solfège awakens the sense of musical pitch and tone relations and the ability to distinguish tone qualities. It develops the ability to listen, the ability to hear, and remember (tonal memory). It should develop a consciousness of sound. Dalcroze used the *fixed* Do syllables.... The earliest solfège study begins to establish C in one's tonal memory. From C, a thorough study is made, hearing and singing the C major scale and the tonal relationships within the scale. All of this is done through the ear, through the muscular sense of singing and through hand positions designating tones of the scale—all before any writing. First the instinct, and then the intellect.[10]

Jaques-Dalcroze's goal in teaching solfège was development of the capacity he called "inner hearing." Through intensive application of theoretical principles in connection with movement, students acquire the ability to hear rhythm patterns, melodic intervals, phrasing, and dynamic nuances in their minds as they look at the musical score. "Mental hearing depends on sensation and memory, so that the art of sight-reading is based on a good receptive condition, on spontaneity of mind, and on certain powers of creative imagination, for intermediate sound-images that serve as bases for reading."[11]

Solfège sessions are a part of each Dalcroze class. Students sing intervals and songs with syllables, and improvise vocally. In learning pitch relationships, students can sing one or more measures aloud and then sing one or more measures silently. Alternatively, when ending one song and beginning another, students can sing the final pitch of the first song and then the beginning pitch of the second, naming the interval between them. The piano is used to test the accuracy of the interval. Many times during a solfège session, students are asked to sing the syllable *do,* which in the European fixed-*do* system is always C. Students are expected to work toward acquiring absolute pitch. Children who are not yet three years old experiment with pitch through body movement, using the space around them to explore highness and lowness. They discover first the wider differences, or the extremes in pitch. In successive lessons smaller intervals are introduced, and they respond to the direction of a melody as they hear it in ascending, descending, or repeating tones. Three-year-olds play musical games in which they match pitches and identify a specific sound whenever it is heard.

In all of this, intensive listening is essential. With it, Dalcroze teachers assume that a good ear can be developed, and the teaching of solfège is directed toward that end. Advanced students sing at sight exercises that correspond in difficulty with those used in conservatories. All scales are sung from C to C (usually with syllables but sometimes with letters). For cases in which students need to use the movable *do* system outside their Dalcroze classes, teachers present it in addition to fixed *do.* In Jaques-Dalcroze's own classes, "After the class had mastered the singing of scales from C to C, a melody would be played and any student could be expected to identify the correct key and sing the scale from C to C."[12]

In a planned sequence of musical learning, note reading is not usually the starting point. An ideal sequence begins with hearing musical sounds, includes some sort of active responses to them, and culminates in note reading and writing. This correctly suggests to children that notation is a means of storing and communicating musical ideas, and is not the heart of the subject. Many activities help prepare children for reading notation. The youngest students listen to scale tones played at the piano and identify them by standing beside cards, numbered one through eight, that are placed in a row on the floor. Children respond to rhythm patterns they hear by marking with crayons on large pieces of paper in a kind of beginning dictation in which dots represent the shortest note values and dashes of varying lengths represent longer note values. Children choose and display cards with quarter notes or eighth notes written on them. These cards are used in various ways to identify their movements, such as walking or running. In a class of older students, a two-measure rhythm pattern is interpreted in movement, students are asked to notate it, and the relationship between the two measures is analyzed. Pairs of students play rhythms on sticks, in simple and complex patterns, striking their own or each other's sticks.

The Dalcroze teaching process begins with natural movements that are a normal part of human life: walking, running, and jumping, for example. Next, students hear rhythms in music that are analogous to these physical movements. They synchronize their movements with the music as they hear it. After a number of such experiences, they are ready to observe in musical notation the rhythm patterns they have experienced. When these patterns are later encountered in a musical score, students can recognize and respond to them because of physiological, as well as intellectual, associations.

The following exercises are examples of the ways in which Jaques-Dalcroze himself taught melody in his classes:

> A melody would be placed on the blackboard with some empty measures which the student would be expected to fill in, improvising, as he sang the melody for the first time.
>
> Another exercise involved writing a melody on the blackboard and as the students sang it through, each phrase was erased upon completion of this initial singing. A student would then be asked to sing the entire melody by memory.[13]

In the study of harmony, Jaques-Dalcroze led his students to sing arpeggiated chords from bass to soprano. A simple chord sequence such as tonic-dominant-tonic could be sung in this way, and then more complex chord sequences could be introduced. In other exercises, students were asked to name specific chords as they heard them. "In chordal singing, students were expected to shift from one part to another upon command. Chordal sequences, placed upon the blackboard, would be played by Jaques-Dalcroze with certain errors which the student was expected to hear and correct. Other chordal sequences were written on the blackboard, erased as they were sung, and then sung by memory."[14]

Improvisation

One of the three basic areas of experience in the Dalcroze plan is improvisation at the piano. The goal of piano improvisation is to give the same freedom at the instrument that students have in whole-body responses to music. This freedom is developed, in part, by assigning exercises in extemporaneous playing, performed in a given tempo and carried out at a brisk pace that does not allow for self-consciousness or negative attitudes. For example, as children are moving freely to music improvised by the teacher, one child may be asked to move toward the piano, improvise a "flute part" in the high register or a "drum part" in the lower as the teacher continues playing in the middle register, all without interruption of the pulse or the movement activity of the rest of the class. Small children often improvise rhythmic patterns on a single tone in descant style, while the teacher plays a sequence of chords. With consistency, students develop improvisation skills and gain a sense of success that contributes to the creative quality of their work.

> The most important abilities developed in Dalcroze training are the abilities to
>
> mirror movements exactly in improvised speech, song, sound, percussion, recorder, piano, and so forth
> accompany any movements, using the same tools
> analyze and perform the underlying meter and beats of given rhythmic movements
> express the varieties of dynamics in a flow of movement
> express the articulation and phrasing of any movement (legato, staccato, portamento)[15]

Improvisation with other instruments and with voice follows a similar pattern. Students play a given measure on percussion instruments and, taking turns, improvise consequent measures following repetitions of the antecedent measure. Children are careful not to lose the basic beat, and no two consequent measures are alike. It is characteristic of the Dalcroze method that spoken commands or signals are given during the process of improvisation. This technique helps to develop intensive listening to all aspects of the music, but it also helps students perfect certain musical skills. For example, while the children are executing a specific rhythmic pattern with their feet, the teacher may call for a contrasting rhythm to be done with the arms.

> Students were encouraged by Dalcroze to improvise their own choice of chords and chord progressions, eventually fitting these into a specific form.... Melodies would be improvised above these chords, with the added complications of change of meter and rhythm, and with modulations. Dance forms, scherzos, rondos, even moods were suggested as forms for improvisation. Advanced students would

improvise together on two pianos, both alternating and in simultaneous performance, requiring a high level of attentive listening, sensitivity, and adjustment to each other. Vocal improvisations among three or more students were also attempted, often quite successfully.[16]

In one exercise, four pitches (such as C, D, E, and F♯) are given. As the teacher plays a harmonic background, students, each entering in turn, sing an improvised rhythmic pattern of two measures using any two of the four pitches. Each student continues to sing his or her pattern until all members of the class have joined. A complex rhythmic and harmonic texture results.

Improvisation carries over into rhythmic movement and solfège. For example, the teacher might play familiar holiday tunes, such as "We Wish You a Merry Christmas," "Happy New Year," and "Happy Hanukkah," and ask students to choose one selection and dance with it. The teacher, improvising at the piano, weaves the three tunes together and observes the original movements created by each of the three groups. In further improvisation, class members are asked to realize one of the tunes in movement while singing another. An advanced student might sing an original melody with syllables, simultaneously playing the rhythm of the melody on a tambourine and improvising appropriate movement.

At the highest level, Dalcroze teachers are expected to be able to improvise in the styles of different composers, showing how the choice of materials, forms, and variational processes reflects the improviser's sensitivity to national qualities of language, religion, dance, and social organization; develop one small musical pattern into a long and fully developed sonata or fugal movement; and remember and reproduce an improvisation after its first performance.[17]

Eurythmics in Special Education

Eurythmics has been recommended for exceptional children—for the talented because it is rich in opportunities for creative and artistic expression, and for the handicapped because it goes to the unconscious level of emotional response and provides for the education of feeling. Jaques-Dalcroze himself worked with both gifted and handicapped students. In Barcelona he taught the visually impaired. On the basis of this experience he commented that sighted children read in the facial expressions of their teachers an attitude of acceptance and approval (or the lack of it), but that blind persons miss this important nonverbal communication. In Eurhythmics, interaction between teacher and class helps to compensate for the loss of usual nonverbal cues. Jaques-Dalcroze suggested that blind persons approach the study of music through the relationships among space, time, and energy. He devised special exercises for developing consciousness of space and of unseen objects. The exercises were arranged according to difficulty, as were those he wrote for general use. He blindfolded some of his students who had normal eyesight and tried these exercises with them. Children as well as adults took part in this blindfold experiment. Jaques-Dalcroze provided written descriptions of twenty-one "Exercises for Developing the Sense of Space and the Muscular Sense" followed by twelve "Exercises for Developing Tactile Sensibility and Muscular Consciousness" and fifteen "Exercises for Developing the Auditory Faculties in their Relation to Space and the Muscular Sense." As a result of his work with blind students and his observation of similar work done by other teachers, Jaques-Dalcroze began to wonder whether sighted people might learn from the blind some important facts about the use of the motor-tactile sense.

The special exercises for the blind can be read in their entirety in the eighth chapter of Jaques-Dalcroze's book, *Eurhythmics, Art and Education*. Some examples follow. In number 8, "Exercises for Developing the Sense of Space and the Muscular Sense," Dalcroze provided the following description:

> Two rows of pupils facing each other. Each pupil in the first row, with outstretched arms, touches the palm of the hand of a pupil in row 2. One step backwards, then again one step forward, clapping the hand that has been released.... Then two steps, three steps, eight steps, twelve steps.... etc.

In number 9 of the same series, he said:

> Two rows, facing each other. Each pupil of row 1 going to his right along row 2, claps, keeping time, the hand of the first pupil opposite him, then the second, third, fourth, etc. The spaces between each pupil should be varied, as also the number of steps to be taken.

Number 1, "Exercises for Developing Tactile Sensibility and Muscular Consciousness," is as follows:

> Realize on the arms of a sighted pupil the crescendos and decrescendos of muscular innervation, in their relation to fullness of gesture—then execute these dynamic nuances oneself. Control is easy to establish if, in moving his arms, the pupil can place the end of his finger on different steps of a ladder or on pegs planted in the wall and serving as guide-marks.

Number 2 of the same series specifies:

> Determine the length of steps, the extent of lunges by the same method. Regulate body balance by means of the muscular sensation created by displacement of the weight of the body.

In number 1, "Exercises for Developing the Auditory Faculties in their Relation to Space and the Muscular Sense":

> The pupils, standing anywhere in the room, guide themselves by the voice of the master. He moves about, uttering a sound or beating a drum from time to time; they walk in the direction of the sound.... The master plays the piano, the pupils, attracted by the sound, make their way towards the piano, to right or left, pass round it, retreat from it during the decrescendo, etc.

And in number 8 of the same series, Jaques-Dalcroze advised the exercise of trying to:

> Distinguish the direction of several sounds uttered simultaneously in various parts of the room.

Historical Development

Born in Vienna to a financially secure Swiss merchant family, Emile and his sister Hélène were fortunate in having their mother Julie support them in their early interest in music. She was a fine music teacher who had studied and taught the philosophy and methods of the educational innovator Pestalozzi. Julie Jaques stimulated her children's love for music. At an early age the children were singing duets and playing four-hand piano pieces. They lived in Vienna, a city of brilliant opera, concerts, and theater. The Jaques family enjoyed them all. Emile responded to these experiences by inventing and performing his own pantomimes and musical plays. At the age of seven he wrote his first march for the piano and the first of more than 600 songs. His love of singing, playing, moving, acting, and creating continued throughout his life, and the integration of all these aspects of music became the impetus for his educational philosophy and practice.

In 1884 Jaques-Dalcroze went to Paris to study music with composers Leo Delibes and Gabriel Fauré and to study acting with members of the Comedie Française. During this time he also studied with Mathis Lussy, the Swiss theorist whose novel theories of rhythm and musical expression contained the seeds of Jaques-Dalcroze's own later rhythmic and expressive processes. In 1886 he accepted a position as assistant conductor at the opera in Algiers. This brought about his first contact with Arabic folk music, which led him to the invention of a new music notation for music of unequal beats and unequal measures. For the first time he realized that there were several worlds of rhythmic expression and that each of these worlds required a unique reading, writing, and performance style.

Jaques-Dalcroze enrolled in the Vienna Conservatory in 1887 to study composition with symphonic composer Anton Bruckner. After graduation he returned to Geneva as an actor, a singer, a conductor, a poet, a composer, a pianist, and an ethnomusicologist.[18]

Essentially, Jaques-Dalcroze's educational theories were stated in two books: *Rhythm, Music and Education* (1921) and *Eurhythmics, Art and Education* (1930). In these, he wrote about the reasons for the development of Eurhythmics. He stressed the three areas of study and pointed out the advantages his system offered to musicians, to those interested in the other arts, and to a school. The earlier book, *Rhythm, Music and Education*, contained essays Jaques-Dalcroze had written between 1898 and 1919. Probably the most important part of this collection was the 1914 statement of the sixty-six exercises Jaques-Dalcroze had developed for teaching rhythmic movement, solfège, and improvisation. *Eurhythmics, Art and Education* was made up of essays written between 1922 and 1925. He included in it a chapter on "Eurhythmics and the Education of the Blind."

Three of the seven chapters in M. E. Sadler's compilation, *The Eurhythmics of Jaques-Dalcroze* (1918), were the work of Jaques-Dalcroze himself. "Rhythm As a Factor in Education" was a reprinted periodical article; "Moving Plastic and Dance" had been taken from the introduction to a book, and the third was titled "Taken From the Lectures of Emile Jaques-Dalcroze." Some definite statements of his educational philosophy were made in these chapters, but the present-day reader meets two problems that obscure all of Jaques-Dalcroze's writings: pre-1930 educational thought, and inadequate translation from French into English.

The *Methode Jaques-Dalcroze* (1907–1914) contained suggested exercises of several kinds, and music to accompany them. In the preface, Jaques-Dalcroze, based on his experience, arrived at several conclusions:

- Eurhythmics cannot be learned exclusively from books.
- the inability of students to hear in their minds the sounds represented by musical notation convinced him that the intellectual study of music is inadequate.
- the success of his ear-training exercises in adult classes led him to believe that similar work should be done with children.
- of the three basic elements in music—melody, rhythm, and dynamics—the latter two are closely related to the physical nature of human beings, and therefore a logical way to study music is through active physical response to it.

Jaques-Dalcroze composed more than six hundred songs for use in Eurhythmics classes. In the ones he wrote for children, the words dealt with familiar childhood experiences. Among his song collections for children were *First Children's Songs and Dances, Children's Songs, New Children's Songs and Dances,* and four volumes of *Action Songs.* For older students, he wrote songs, exercises in solfège, piano music, and music for violin and piano.

In 1950, at the age of 85, Emile Jaques-Dalcroze died. His legacy to the musical world includes:

1. Three major books, plus numerous shorter discussions on movement and music theory. In addition to the original French language, translations of various articles and books are found in English, German, Italian, and Russian
2. Thirty-nine musical pageants (spectacles), including one opera
3. One hundred eight orchestral works, including transcriptions of sections of the various pageants
4. Eighty-five chamber works for many instrumental combinations
5. One hundred twenty-five piano pieces
6. Over 1,000 songs with piano accompaniment, including action songs, songs for children, folklike Swiss songs, and art songs

7. Seventy-five songs with orchestral accompaniment
8. Over 200 unaccompanied choral pieces
9. One hundred seventy-five choral pieces with piano accompaniment
10. Two hundred choral pieces with orchestral accompaniment
11. Three concertos for violin and orchestra
12. Two smaller works, one for violin and one for flute, both with orchestral accompaniment[19]

Rhythmic movement was the basic instructional procedure in the Dalcroze approach to music education, so Jaques-Dalcroze's ideas were taught (as dance is taught) by means of personal instruction rather than through written materials. During his lifetime, the originator of Eurhythmics gave his personal approval to those he felt were qualified to teach his method; as a result, the spread of Eurhythmics outside the country of its origin depended on a few specially trained teachers. Those who insisted that the method be used in a pure form and in its entirety found that the public schools could not provide time or space for it. Other teachers adapted some of the procedures to the needs of their classes. Still others learned specific ideas or instructional devices and began to use them without knowing their source. For example, the use of walking and running movements to represent quarter- and eighth-note values became fairly widespread in the United States.

The first American to receive a Dalcroze certificate was Lucy Duncan Hall, who taught for many years at New York University. The Dalcroze School of Music in New York City was founded in 1915. The Cleveland Institute of Music was first in the United States to grant a degree in Eurhythmics, and the first permanent Department of Eurhythmics was begun at Carnegie-Mellon University. The influence of Dalcroze's ideas could be found in the basal series published for school use, beginning in 1936 and becoming steadily more widespread.

The Dalcroze Society of America can be contacted through Marta Sanchez, Director of the Dalcroze Training Center, Carnegie-Mellon University, Pittsburgh, PA 15213.

Notes

1. Arthur F. Becknell, "A History of the Development of Dalcroze Eurhythmics in the United States and Its Influence on the Public School Music Program," (Doctoral dissertation, University of Michigan, 1970), 13.

2. Jack Dobbs, "Some Great Music Educators: Emile Jaques-Dalcroze," *Music Teacher* 47, No. 8 (August 1968), 13.

3. Emile Jaques-Dalcroze, "Teaching Music Through Feeling," *Etude* 39 (June 1921), 368.

4. Jo Pennington, *The Importance of Being Rhythmic: A Study of the Principles of Dalcroze Eurhythmics Applied to General Education and to the Arts of Music, Dancing, and Acting*. Based on and adapted from *Rhythm, Music and Education* by Emile Jaques-Dalcroze; with an introduction by Walter Damrosch (New York; G. P. Putnam's Sons, 1925), 26–27. Used by permission.

5. Dobbs, "Some Great Music Educators," 13.

6. Emile Jaques-Dalcroze, "Eurhythmics and Its Implications," trans. Frederic Rothwell, *Musical Quarterly* 16 (July 1930), 358.

7. Emile Jaques-Dalcroze, *Eurhythmics, Art and Education* (London: Chatto and Windus, 1930), 110–11.

8. Dalcroze later discarded the term "Rhythmic Counterpoint" and substituted "Complementary Rhythm." The new term suggests that the second rhythm pattern *completes* or complements the first.

9. Pennington, 14–26.

10. Virginia Hoge Mead, "An Appraisal of the Dalcroze Method," report of an article from the Ohio Music Educators Association *Triad*.

11. Dalcroze, *Eurhythmics, Art, and Education*, trans. Frederick Rothwell, 107.

12. Becknell, "A History," 16.

13. Becknell, 16.

14. Becknell, 16–17.

15. Choksy, Lois, Robert Abramson, Avon Gillespie, and David Woods, *Teaching Music in the Twentieth Century* (Englewood Cliffs, NJ: Prentice-Hall, 1986), 62.

16. Becknell, "A History," 18.

17. Choksy et al., *Teaching Music*, 28–29.

18. Jaques-Dalcroze, *Rhythm, Music and Education*, trans. Harold F. Rubenstein, abridged reprint ed. (London and Whitstable: The Riverside Press, 1967).

19. Becknell, "A History," 12.

The Timelessness of Jaques-Dalcroze's Approach

by Arthur F. Becknell

The method of teaching music developed by Emile Jaques-Dalcroze has gained wide acceptance throughout the United States, especially at the elementary school level. The influence of this man's ideas in music textbook series and in specific classroom activities in the 1930s has been reported in an earlier publication.[1] Later writings, such as Elsa Findlay's[2] book, document in pictures and in written exercises extensive use of Jaques-Dalcroze's principles at the elementary level. Less well known, however, is the increased use of the musical principles of eurhythmics, solfège, and improvisation at upper levels of instruction in the public schools and at the college/university level.

On a personal note, I was first introduced to the eurhythmics of Jaques-Dalcroze as an undergraduate. The instruction I received made a profound impression on my early years of teaching middle and high school vocal music. As I moved to college level teaching that included music education methods classes and supervision of student teachers, I became aware of how much I was still using these ideas as both teacher and performer—a realization that led to my completing certification training at the New York Dalcroze School of Music.

One of the benefits of the ideas of Jaques-Dalcroze is their complete adaptability at any level of musical instruction. From the student's point of view, meter or time signature, for example, will be sensed first as simply the organization of beats around an accent (Jaques-Dalcroze's definition). As the student matures musically, and as physical experiences in movement with the music become more internalized, he or she senses meter in relation to the note values that are part of the musical phrase. The understanding of phrase through movement principles is enhanced at a more advanced level by experiencing the beat, its organization (meter), and the shape of the phrase in both its pitch and rhythmic aspects. Other advanced concepts of Eurhythmics, such as quick reactions, canon, diminution/augmentation, and metric transformation, can certainly be of benefit to any student's total learning situation in developing keen mental discipline, muscular control, and heightened analytical skills.

Once these basic principles are established, students can apply them to the performance of music. Such simple problems as inaccurate subdivision, in simple meter, of a quarter note into two eighth notes can be studied individually or in groups by stepping the quarter pulse while tapping the eighth subdivision. If space does not permit this type of movement, the students could remain seated and feel the quarter pulse by either raising their heels off the floor (better than just tapping the toe) or by a slight swaying motion. The teacher should maintain a steady beat at the keyboard, with a hand drum, or perhaps with a metronome. When the quarter and eighth note relationships are firmly established, a student could then sing or play a rhythmic phrase while other members of the class continue with both the steady quarter pulse and a light tapping of the eighth note subdivision. Another movement exercise might involve group "swaying" of the pulse beat in compound meter (the dotted quarter) while patterns built on subdivisions are clapped or spoken (using either a text, if available, or a neutral syllable such as "loo.")

The goal of all Jaques-Dalcroze's principles is to give the student a musical "experience," not just to present ideas or principles separated from the music. Rather than seeking an intellectual understanding of musical notation, Eurhythmics builds a physical feeling for the musical phrase. As movement ideas are developed, attention is always given to this phrase feeling.

Regardless of the length of the phrase, there should be some indication in the movement pattern that the phrase has been completed and that it is either repeated or that a new phrase begins. This is easily demonstrated by a slight change in the direction of movement by the student. Even in larger classes, it is possible to move a given phrase with a sense of direction or "flow," and then indicate the change as the new phrase begins. The ability to "visualize" one's phrase movement in relation to others in the class prepares the student for the aural experience of relating his or her musical line to the musical lines that others are producing in the ensemble experience. At a more advanced level, having two performers show their musical lines in movement patterns can create a totally new concept of ensemble playing or singing. For example: what relationship exists between the phrase movement of a piano part and the vocal line in an art song? Between the phrase movement of a piano part and the instrumental line in a sonata?

Solfège-Rhythmique

An exciting adjunct to the traditional approach to music theory is provided by Jaques-Dalcroze's Solfège-Rhythmique. In this system, pitch intervals of the scale are presented with specific rhythmic durations. For example, the dichord (interval of the second) is sung in $\frac{4}{4}$ meter on the quarter pulse.

Major seconds (whole steps) are presented first, and minor seconds (half steps) are added when the students are prepared to hear the difference. During the fourth-beat rest, a new pitch is given and the interval is then sung from that pitch. After the students have drilled these two intervals, the teacher can indicate by a hand gesture or verbal cue that they are to sing either a major or a minor second, and the two intervals can be intermixed.

Trichords are added next, singing through the dichord using the pitch relationships already established. The rhythm of the trichord is in $\frac{5}{4}$ meter with the following rhythm:

When working with the C major scale (the key of *do* in the fixed *do* system), the pitches C-D-E (encompassing two major seconds) form a Type I trichord. The Type II trichord consists of the pitches C-D-E♭ (a major second followed by a minor second). The Type III trichord consists of the pitches C-Db-Eb (a minor second followed by a major second). As students gain facility with these three Types of trichords, and as they become accustomed to the entire scale, patterns can be introduced to intermix the various types. In the following example, the pattern continues upward, completing the scale. C-D-E (Type I), D-E-F (Type II), E-F-G (Type III), F-G-A (Type I), G-A-B (Type I), and A-B-C (Type II). Further explication of this system can be found in the recent publication, *Teaching Music in the Twentieth Century.*[3]

The tetrachord completes this aspect of Jaques-Dalcroze's "basics" by using the following rhythm, also in 5/4 meter.

Again working in the key of C Major, the pitches of a Type I tetrachord would be C-D-E-F (containing the intervals of major second, major second, and minor second). Other tetrachords are formed by chromatic alteration: Type II (C-D-E♭ -F), Type III (C-D♭ -E♭ -F), and Type IV (C♭ -D♭ -E♭ -F). Larger intervals are formed by combining dichords, trichords, and tetrachords. An interesting benefit of this approach to the study of music theory is that students can feel the rhythmic value of a pitch interval, thus assisting in harmonic analysis. For example, when this chord is played,

the student feels the energy of the fourth on the bottom, identifying the $^6_4$ position of the triad (second inversion of the chord). The students learn other inversions in relation to the rhythmic values of the pitch intervals.

The first chord (A♭ in first inversion) would be heard as a Type II trichord with a Type II tetrachord on top. The second chord (D7 in third inversion) would be heard as a major second dichord with a Type I trichord (two major seconds) followed by a Type III trichord (minor second and major second).

Improvisation and Contemporary Music

Improvisation, the third area of Jaques-Dalcroze's approach, can be one of the most creative and natural aspects of the musical experience. His philosophy was that theory should follow practice, that students should not be taught rules until they have had experiences that give rise to these rules. Therefore, he considered improvisation an integral part of the study of music and encouraged keyboard, body and vocal inventiveness. Improvisation should be used at all levels of musical training to develop freedom of expression in the individual.

The years have not dulled the vitality and efficacy of the ideas developed by this great man. As he was always searching for new ways to understand and present music to his students, so his principles can be expanded to encompass ideas of contemporary music. Unusual metric patterns and unusual rhythmic relationships can be worked out in movement in the same way that the simple relationship of eighth notes to quarter notes is done for the beginner. Unusual pitch relationships, such as atonal patterns, can be drilled with the Solfège-Rhythmique exercises. Jaques-Dalcroze left an enormous legacy to the teaching of music when he died at the age of eighty-five. One of the exciting aspects of this legacy is that it continues to be a vital influence in the teaching and performing of music some forty years after his death. The extension of his principles is illustrated in the many workshops being offered from coast to coast and in the formation of local Dalcroze chapters for the promulgation of these ideas. The Institut Jaques-Dalcroze in Geneva, Switzerland, has authorized additional training schools (with clearly defined standards) so that the number of these schools has doubled in just the last twenty years.[4]

Notes

1. Arthur F. Becknell, "A History of the Development of Dalcroze Eurhythmics in the United States and Its Influence on the Public School Music Program" (Doctoral dissertation, University of Michigan, 1970).

2. Elsa Findlay, *Rhythm and Movement: Applications of Dalcroze Eurhythmics* (Princeton, NJ: The Birchtree Group, 1971).

3. Lois Choksy, Robert M. Abramson, Avon E. Gillespie, and David Woods. *Teaching Music in the Twentieth Century* (Englewood Cliffs, NJ: Prentice-Hall, 1986), 58–60.

4. Statistics from 1970 are presented in Arthur Becknell's "A History of the Development of Dalcroze Eurhythmics."

The Importance of Rhythmic Training in Music Education

by Annabelle S. Joseph

Teaching [music] should be concerned primarily with stimulating, cultivating and preserving a heightened sense of rhythm. Any complication in meter must be heard and felt.[1] It isn't mathematics that solves the problem. It is the aural image plus its physical counterpart—a progression toward a goal—that establishes the solution.[2]

Emile Jaques-Dalcroze (1865–1950), a Swiss musician and educator, developed a unique approach to the study of music based on rhythm as the crucial link coordinating what we hear with what we do. This approach, known as Eurhythmics, is a three-part process for musical growth integrating rhythmic movement, ear training, and improvisation. Music is abstract; we hear it moving through time. Movement is concrete; we see it moving through space. By connecting listening with moving, Jaques-Dalcroze hoped to clarify abstract music concepts. His experiments led to the discovery that rhythmic movement in response to intelligent and sensitive listening develops both the tonal and the rhythmic senses, thereby enhancing the understanding, the enjoyment, and the performance of music.

Although the tonal and rhythmic aspects of music are perceived simultaneously, research shows that tonal and rhythmic aptitude are not necessarily correlated. Each requires an appropriate form of training. The tonal part of music is perceived aurally; rhythm is sensed through our muscles. Most music programs train the ear to refine its perception of pitch. Unfortunately, few train the muscles to refine their perception of rhythm. Our sense of movement in music comes from intuition, experience, knowledge, and an understanding of time (beat/pulse) and timing (time/space between beats). Great comedians are known for their sense of timing; the same is true of great musicians. A perfect sense of rhythm, if it could be measured, might be rarer than perfect pitch.

The most basic element in music to which we respond is pulsation or beat. It is the organizer of the melodic line. The capacity for building understanding and enjoyment of music is founded on the ability to find, maintain, externalize, and internalize a steady beat and patterns of beats. This may seem a simple task, but many children (and many adults) cannot perform this task with ease and accuracy. Rhythmic response to aural input can be compared to the game "telephone," in which a message is whispered from one person to another until the last participant speaks the message aloud. The message often changes dramatically during transmission.

Rhythmic response to music input is the result of signals that the brain transmits through the central nervous system to the muscles. As in the telephone game, the message often gets garbled during transmission so that the output does not match the input. Everyone has a transmission system, but some work more efficiently than others. Since improved coordination is a result of rhythmic training, and coordination is necessary for efficient and effective performance in any area, rhythmic training is beneficial to everyone.

Work with Dalcroze techniques is valuable at any age, but ideally it should begin in early childhood. Dalcroze classes for young children are designed to awaken musical instinct and imagination and to sensitize children to the varied and multilevel cues in music prior to formal instruction. The lessons are based on elements of music that can be demonstrated through movement, such as tempo, dynamics, accents, beat, patterns, meter, phrasing, form, and style. These elements are explored in a spiral manner that requires ever more sophisticated levels of response as the students advance in their ability to hear tonal and rhythmic subtleties in music. A transfer of learning takes place as students manipulate the same elements in different compositions. Although the basic elements of music are inseparable, students can focus on each element individually, providing the teacher with immediate feedback for reinforcing, refining or restructuring the material presented.

When introducing movement activities at any age, movement exploration should precede rhythmic movement work—just as sound exploration should precede vocal work. Students should have a vocabulary of movement before attempting to adjust movement to music. Since movement excites children, activities should be paced carefully. At first, music should be played at a moderate tempo, so that the children are able to control their movement. Once they are at ease in moderate speeds, faster tempi can be introduced. Slow speeds need careful attention because of the control required to achieve a balance of time, space, and energy. It is better to let the children find their own movement than to demonstrate for them. The tendency to imitate is very strong; individual initiative should always be encouraged and acknowledged.

Children should hear quality music of all genres and from many cultures. Much of this music is accessible only on recordings, but teachers must use recordings carefully because the medium limits possibilities for isolating and repeating specific parts of a composition. For this reason, eurhythmics teachers are trained to use the piano for improvisation—a practice that gives them flexibility in presenting, isolating, and reinforcing concepts.

Both improvised and composed music are used in a Eurhythmics class. A valuable source of composed music for illustrating specific concepts is upper elementary- and intermediate-level piano music.[3] To elicit a musical response, improvisation (whether on percussion or melodic instruments) should be as musical as possible.

A Dalcroze class is like a game of "Listen/Show/Tell." There is no right or wrong response—there are only more or less appropriate responses. After sufficient experience in moving to music, teachers should encourage children to verbalize about the qualities in the music that caused their responses. They should word questions to the students carefully in an attempt to elicit answers that require critical thinking. Some children may excel in movement while others may excel in analysis. Knowing this, the teacher can pair children accordingly so that they learn from each other.

Introducing Rhythm Concepts to Children

Listen to:	Respond with:
Sound vs silence	Movement when music is heard; no movement during silence. This is preparation for the study of phrasing and articulation.
Duration and intensity of a sound	Movement with appropriate use of time, space, and energy to show the length and intensity of a sound. Movements performed in response to the duration and sound quality of contrasting instruments (such as a triangle and a woodblock) can illustrate this.

Tempo/Mood/Style	Spontaneous movement to awaken imagination and sensitivity to the expressive/interpretive components of music.
Dynamics	Movement with appropriate energy in response to various levels and gradations of dynamics such as forte, piano, crescendo, decrescendo and sforzando. Dynamics is an integral part of music that provides a constant source for demonstrating attentive listening.
Phrases	Movement in place or through space, showing the beginning and end of each musical thought.
Accelerando/Ritardando	Repetitive movements (such as hammering, swinging, marching, or jogging) in which the space between motions decreases as the tempo gets faster and increases as the tempo gets slower.
Pulsation/Beat	Movement in place or through space following a steady beat. Students at all ages and levels of musical development must attend constantly to the concept of a steady beat. This must be experienced in a variety of tempi.
Meter	Organizing a pattern of movements to illustrate how beats are grouped.
Proportional relationships	Finding movements that represent the given beat and movements that can be performed twice as slow or twice as fast as the

given beat. The class can be divided into three groups so that each group responds to one of three proportional note values such as quarter, eighth, and half notes. This proportional relationship should be experienced in different tempi. Proportional durations such as note values that are twice as fast or twice as slow as a given beat should not be emphasized until children can demonstrate the ability to move proportionally. Students need much physical experience with this concept before the teacher gives theoretical explanations.

Rhythm patterns

Movements that show the duration of each note value in a pattern.

Beat and pattern

Coordinating movements to show both beat and pattern. Before commingling beat and pattern, children can perform a pattern such as a skip or a gallop until signaled by the teacher to "change." This can signal a shift from moving the pattern to clapping it. When this is mastered, the signal can be used to indicate a shift from moving the pattern to clapping the beat. Combining both these ideas, the children can step the beat and clap the pattern.

Grouping rhythm patterns into phrases by repetition, contrast, sequence, and development

Movements that illustrate each of these compositional devices.

Grouping phrases into larger structures for form

Movements clearly showing the structural groupings such as phrases, periods, and sections within a composition.

41

Emile Jaques-Dalcroze spent much of his life experimenting with musical rhythm and its relation to movement as a means for enlivening and enhancing the study of music. His experiments culminated in the development of eurhythmics, a unique approach to the process of musical development that puts rhythmic training at the center of the process. The lack of a sense of rhythmic flow in many music students at all levels underscores the significance of Jaques-Dalcroze's pioneering work. Since there have been no long-term studies of how Dalcroze education affects developing musicianship, it seems reasonable to ask "What would happen if Eurhythmics were an integral part of the music curriculum?" Teachers who believe that a sense of rhythmic flow is important for understanding, enjoying, and performing music may want to attempt to answer this question by exploring the Dalcroze approach to a musical education.

Certification is required to teach Dalcroze Eurhythmics. There are three levels of Dalcroze certification: certificate, license, and diploma. The diploma is obtainable only at the Institut Jaques-Dalcroze in Geneva, Switzerland. Dalcroze programs leading to the certificate and the license can be pursued at four training centers in the United States: Carnegie Mellon University in Pittsburgh, Dalcroze School of Music in New York, Longy School of Music in Cambridge, Massachusetts, and Manhattan School of Music in New York.

Dalcroze educators are featured at international music conferences and they present courses and workshops throughout the world. Many colleges and universities in the United States offer regular courses in Dalcroze work, some of which carry credit toward certification. A list of certified Dalcroze educators is available from the Dalcroze Society of America, an organization of Dalcroze teachers and others interested in their work, affiliated with the Fédération Internationale des Enseignants de Rythmique (FIER), a worldwide association of Dalcroze teachers with headquarters in Geneva, Switzerland.[4] The Society sponsors a biennial national conference and regional conferences in the intervening years, and has a scholarship fund to help train future Dalcroze teachers.

Notes

1. Abby Whiteside, *Indispensables of Piano Playing*. (New York: Charles Scribner's Sons, 1955), 5.

2. Whiteside, 131.

3. Some of these sources are listed in Annabelle S. Joseph's "A Dalcroze Approach to Music Learning in Kindergarten" (Doctoral dissertation, Carnegie Mellon University, 1982).

4. For more information, contact Dr. Annabelle Joseph, Music Department, Carnegie Mellon University, Pittsburgh, PA 15213.

Eurhythmics, Aural Training and Creative Thinking: The Dalcroze Pedagogy for Children

by Patricia Shehan Campbell

The principles developed by Emile Jacques-Dalcroze provide the single most complete system of rhythmic training to appear in the twentieth century.[1] His approach to musical understanding through eurhythmics was intended for the development of immediate physical responses to rhythmic stimuli. Jaques-Dalcroze described eurhythmics as a necessary experience with music through movement that would develop the muscular rhythms and nervous sensibility, and that would lead to the capacity to discriminate even slight gradations of duration, time, intensity, and phrasing.[2] He felt that through rhythmic movement, children could begin to think and express themselves more musically. His missionary zeal, and that of his disciples, established Eurhythmics as a credible pedagogy for both children and adults in much of the modern world.

While tribute has been paid to the Eurhythmics component of the Dalcroze approach, the tripartite nature of his system of developing musicianship is less frequently recognized. Jaques-Dalcroze believed that children are musical when they possess "an ensemble of physical and spiritual resources and capacities, comprising, on the one hand, ear, voice, and consciousness of sound, and on the other hand, the whole body (bone, muscle, and nervous systems), and the consciousness of bodily rhythm."[3] He viewed the study of rhythm as an awakening of the whole organism to music, and rhythmic movement as the foundation for raising each child's musical sensitivity to its fullest potential. While Eurhythmics was the core of his approach, Dalcroze advocated aural training through solfège and creative improvisation as "part and parcel" of his system of comprehensive musicianship.

Despite his teachings, solfège and improvisation have been frequently perceived as adjuncts rather than integral parts of the approach. To ignore these components is to misrepresent the Dalcroze approach and to distort the method. Eurhythmics itself has been frequently misinterpreted as being based on the idea of "movement-for-movement's sake"—a technique that falls somewhere between physical conditioning exercises and the art of the dance. These limited experiences, while of benefit to children's motor development, seldom ripen their conceptual understanding of melody, rhythm, texture, and form. Jaques-Dalcroze espoused a more thorough approach to musicianship in which the child's body, voice, and creative intellect work together in perceiving and expressing music. In defining the composite nature of the Dalcroze system, the integration of aural and kinesthetic factors will be noted in suggestions for the infusion of movement (eurhythmics), song (solfège and solfège-rhythmique) and creative improvisation in the elementary classroom.

The Marriage of Movement and Song

Movement and song may well be one of the most natural alliances in the repertoire of human behaviors. Children, in particular, are inclined to rock, step, or even skip as they chant and sing. Just as the babbling of infants leads to speech and song, their rhythmic bouncing and swaying movements are gradually replaced by controlled gestures of isolated body parts, complex combinations of movement, and choreographic sequences that they initiate and transmit.[4] It is thus no wonder that Emile Jaques-Dalcroze sought to develop students' inner hearing through the natural relationship between movement and song as found in the techniques of solfège and solfège-rhythmique, or "rhythmic singing".

At the Geneva Conservatory, the master pedagogue accepted students into his solfège class following a year of Eurhythmics training, intended to awaken the students' bodies to the capacity to respond physically to music. Jaques-Dalcroze then led his students to an understanding of pitch and pitch relationships through a series of vocal exercises. Beginning with "rhythmic gymnastics" that activated the diaphragm, lungs, and articulatory functions of the mouth and tongue, students were soon singing scales in dichord and trichord arrangements, in canon with the teacher, at double and half the speed of the original statement, and alternating "silent" internal song and singing aloud on cue. For Jaques-Dalcroze, the intent of solfège class was to teach students "to hear, and to reproduce mentally, melodies in all keys."[5]

For children in American schools, Dalcroze solfège can serve as a model for nurturing musical understanding through experiences that combine vocal and kinesthetic expression. Aural skills are activated each time children listen to themselves or to others as they sing. When children are directed to focus their attention on specific pitches, patterns, and phrases within the context of a song or scale, they are well on their way to more discriminating listening. When they are presented with opportunities to combine song with movement, their resulting bimodal activity reinforces the musical concept and thus sharpens their aural perception skills. Through the Dalcroze solfège, children experience rather than deliberate over the theoretical underpinnings of a song. They sing more musically as a result, converting experience to intellectual understanding and expressive performance.

The Dalcroze approach to aural training through solfège is flexible, and can be easily adjusted to the developmental level of the child, to various songs and styles, and to a host of musical concepts. While Jaques-Dalcroze himself preferred the fixed *do* system, the movable *do* system, or numbers, letters, or even neutral syllables can be substituted. Regardless of the vocables employed, the principle remains unchanged: children who combine listening with singing and movement can thus comprehend the essence of the music. As participants fully engaged in the "musical innards" of a song's melody or rhythm, they are at once active listeners and performers. A sequence of solfège activities, along with associated eurhythmics and improvisation experiences, is found in the accompanying lesson plan on "Sing Together" for children ages 8–9 in the third or fourth grades. The lesson illustrates a playful collection of solfège techniques suitable for children. A wealth of the Dalcroze solfège is also available for exploration at more advanced levels of musical training.

A Solfège Sequence for Aural Training

Lesson Concepts:
  do–mi–sol
  ti–do–re–do
  re–mi–fa–mi
  major scale

$^6_8$: ♫♩, ♩ ♪, ♩.

1. As the teacher sings the song, the children sway or swing to the dotted-quarter-note pulse (♩.).
2. As the teacher sings, the children swing their arms in a duple-meter conducting gesture. (Such conducting gestures can be encouraged throughout listening and singing experiences.)
3. Children learn the song in rote fashion, two measures at a time, in an "interrupted canon" that follows the teacher. As they listen and then sing each phrase, they continue to conduct the dotted-quarter-note pulse (♩.).
4. As the teacher keeps the pulse on a drum, piano, or xylophone, the children sing the song, stepping the pulse and conducting the meter.
5. Children begin singing. On a predetermined cue (a woodblock tap or the word "change"), they sing silently until they hear the cue again, at which point they return to singing aloud.
6. As children sing, they draw the melodic contour in space. The teacher asks them to decide which of the three four-measure phrases is highest and which is lowest. They map the melodic contour in space again while several children draw it on the board. They then follow their "blackboard score" as a guide while singing.
7. The teacher asks "where is the home pitch?" and the children respond by singing the tonic or "F" (on "loo," "do," "fa," "one," "F," or some other designated syllable). Children are then directed to listen to the teacher sing and to clap lightly each time the "home pitch" sounds. They may also wish to find a home space (this may be a carpet square or a tile block), staying in it when the tonic is sung and moving away from it when other pitches are sounded.
8. As the teacher plays the song on a pitched instrument, children substitute *do* or another designated syllable each time the tonic appears. Children may sing all other pitches on a neutral non-interfering syllable; this ensures that the melodic line and musical flow are retained.

46

9. Steps 6 and 7 are repeated for *mi* and *sol*.
10. The teacher introduces *ti, re,* and *fa* as passing tones, stable neighbors just below and above *do* and *mi.* He or she sings measures 3–4 and 7–8, passages that contain neighboring pitches; the children echo the teacher's singing.

The major scale concept can be extended with the following ideas:

- To discover whole- and half-step relationships within the major scale, direct the children to step widely between whole steps and to step in "baby steps" between *ti* and *do* and *mi* and *fa* as they sing. They may line up, or simply choose their home space from which they can step the scale, facing home again as they step the descending scale.

- Children may also sing the major scale and song phrases that contain adjacent pitches (such as *ti–do–re–do, re–mi–fa–mi*) by using their hands, opening wide for whole steps and closing for half steps.

- Children form a line of eight across, facing the class. Each one steps forward from the line as his or her designated pitch is sung. The spatial relationship between *ti* and *do* and between *mi* and *fa* is represented as these children lean toward each other, hook elbows, or put their arms across the other's shoulders. The "human scale" may challenge the class by rearranging the half and whole steps for the remainder of the children to sing.

- Sing the scale, using various rhythmic patterns:

11. As the children continue to conduct the pulse, the teacher sings an improvised two-measure phrase, combining the pitches and rhythms of the song; the children echo his or her singing.
12. Once a tonal vocabulary is firmly implanted, children are offered an opportunity to improvise their own two-measure phrases, which are followed by the group's echo-response. The resulting "group song" should flow without pause; the children can be arranged in a circle, and when the first child's song has been repeated by the group, the next child follows immediately with a new phrase.
13. In a canon activity, the teacher asks the children to listen to two-measure phrases and then to step the rhythm of the melody. (Phrases can be extracted from the song or improvised.) Once they are comfortable with their movement, children can be directed to move following phrases that incorporate *do, mi,* or *sol,* but to freeze when a phrase utilizes a neighboring tone.

Note that while there are many canonic experiences in this lesson, singing the song as a round is not one of them. Many third-grade children are not developmentally prepared to sing simultaneous yet independent melodies. Still, these experiences demonstrate the principle of canon for later experiences with harmony.

Creative Thinking Through Dalcroze Improvisation

Like song and movement, creative behavior in music is a human phenomenon that knows no cultural boundaries.[6] Musical thought is expressed through two processes: composition—music that is consciously thought-out and often notated, and improvisation—the spontaneous creation of music that relates to a model but is more simply and rapidly conceived.[7] Creative thinking in music is not a phenomenon limited to adults; it occurs in children from an early age. They begin during the preschool years with personalized and individualistic treatments of tonal and rhythmic elements in their invented songs, and progress to an increasingly predictable use of culturally conventional patterns through the primary grades.[8] Despite the great potential that children have for creative thinking in music, however, they are rarely afforded the opportunity to express themselves through spontaneous music-making in their music classes.

Jaques-Dalcroze advocated experiences for children in improvisation as an absolute measure of musical understanding, a true synthesis of earlier experiences. He explained that eventual virtuosity on an instrument "should rest on a joint physical and intellectual basis, demonstrating the inseparability of body from soul." [9] Mastery of an instrument is not a matter of agility and power, he observed, but of the acquisition of the arts of musical "breathing" and interpretation, or of balancing one's own temperament with the intentions of the composers. According to Dalcroze, eurhythmics experiences develop the muscular mechanism necessary for instrumental performance, while solfège study enables the ear to compare the notation to the actual sound on the instrument. In addition, preliminary aural training provides children with a rich vocabulary of musical ideas that can be retrieved with great speed and spontaneity.

Dalcroze supported the development of improvisational skills at the piano, but the principle of creative thinking in music can aptly be applied to any instrument, to vocal improvisation, and to expressive movement.[10] By providing experiences for children in American schools, classroom instruments offer rich potential for creative expression. Pitched and nonpitched percussion instruments, from hand drums and woodblocks to the Orff xylophones and metallophones, recorders, keyboards, and guitars are useful tools for expressing musical ideas. From the most fundamental "making up" of a rhythmic pulse to accompany "marching soldiers," to the creation of a musical dialogue between instruments, to abstract communications of feeling through a more extensive musical structure, the

Dalcroze approach to improvisation can be adapted to children at every level of their musical development.

Suggestions for the development of creative thinking in music through Dalcroze techniques are offered in the accompanying list of ideas. The integration of eurhythmics and solfège reflects once again the composite nature of the Dalcroze pedagogy. The lesson activities, broadly suitable for children in the elementary grades, are intended to be carefully tailored by the teacher to meet the demands of a particular group or lesson. The more experienced musician who is searching for the challenge of improvisation exercises for the voice, piano, or other instruments should consult the complete table of improvisation exercises provided by Jaques-Dalcroze.[11]

Improvisation as Creative Thinking in Music

- *Canon:* In preparation for improvisation, the teacher plays short phrases that are immediately imitated by the children on their instruments. The phrases begin with rhythms only. The teacher then moves on to present scales and short, simple passages from familiar songs, followed by unfamiliar phrases of increasing length.
- *Elements for musical expression:* Using voice, drum, woodblock, finger cymbals, or xylophone, the children express an assortment of musical ideas such as long and slow or short and quick, loud or soft, becoming louder or softly fading, jumping and bouncing or gliding and sliding, high or low, or high and descending or low and ascending. As some children sing or play, others move expressively to the durations, pitch register, and quality of articulation.
- *Musical dialogue:* In a frame of 4 or 8 beats, the teacher plays an antecedent phrase, followed by an improvised consequent phrase of matching length. The pulse should remain steady, the tempo unchanged. Once the model has been set, children respond to the teacher's musical questions as a group: on instruments, vocally, and through movement. To provide further practice, partners can create dialogue with each other.
- *From rhythm to melody:* Children are given a rhythmic pattern, to which they invent a melody. (Alternately, children may determine a rhythm for organizing a given set of pitches). They may extend the melodic or rhythmic unit to a full-fledged song through repetition, contrast, and variation.
- *Changing patterns:* Children begin with a rhythm or melody, repeating it until the teacher commands "change," at which point they spontaneously invent a new phrase.
- *Conductor's choice:* The children work in pairs; one child acts as the conductor while the other improvises rhythms or melodies—freely, but nonetheless following the conductor's gestures for tempo and dynamic nuance. The conductor may add to the conventional gestures through full body movement.

- *Storytelling through music:* The children tell a selected story through narration, music, and movement. Some children act the parts of the characters, while others assemble themselves in an ensemble for providing not only sound effects but leitmotifs for assorted characters, places, and ideas. Maurice Sendak's "Where the Wild Things Are," Arthur Yorink's "Bravo Minski," Jurg Obrist's "The Miser Who Wanted the Sun," and Mark Taylor's "The Fisherman and the Goblet" are rich with potential for musical interpretation.

The pedagogy of Emile Jaques-Dalcroze offers a variety of techniques for developing the children's abilities in three essential areas: their musical, intellectual, and physical capacities. His mission was to develop (through eurhythmics, aural training, and creative improvisation) a comprehensive musicianship that could be presented to professional and student musicians of every age and level of experience. While his techniques are practiced in the great conservatories of the world—and are in fact embedded in the curricular plans of many school music programs—the full flowering of his approach remains to be realized. The musical challenges are real, but the threefold benefits to children and their teachers are rewarding beyond measure.

Notes

Special thanks to a number of American Dalcroze master-teachers whose musicianship has invigorated and inspired me over the years: Anne Farber, Herb Henke, Annabelle Joseph, Virginia Hogge Mead, Lisa Parker, Marta Sanchez, and Julia Schnebly-Black.—Patricia Shehan Campbell

1. Campbell, Patricia Shehan. "Rhythmic Movement and Public School Music Education: Conservative and Progressive Views in the Formative Years" (Paper presented at the MENC National Biennial In-Service Conference, March, 1990.)

2. Emile Jaques-Dalcroze, *Eurhythmics, Arts and Education,* trans. F. Rothwell (New York: A.S. Barnes and Co., 1930).

3. Emile Jaques-Dalcroze, *Rhythm, Music and Education,* rev. ed., trans. H. Rubenstein (London: The Dalcroze Society, 1967), 36.

4. Helmut Moog, *The Musical Experience of the Pre-school Child,* trans. C. Clarke, (London: Schott, 1976); Patricia Shehan Campbell, "The Childsong Genre: A Comparison of Songs By and For Children." *Update* 7, no. 3 (1989), 18–20; Fernanda Magno Prim, "The Importance of Girl's Singing Games in Music and Motor Education," *Canadian Music Educator* 30, no. 2 (May 1989), 115–23; Carol Merrill-Mirsky, *Eeny Meeny Pepsadeeny: Ethnicity and Gender in Children's Musical Play.* (Doctoral dissertation. Ann Arbor, Michigan: University Microfilms 8826013, 1988).

5. Jaques-Dalcroze, *Rhythm, Music and Education,* 65.

6. Campbell, Patricia Shehan, "Crosscultural Perspectives of Musical Creativity."

Music Educators Journal 76, no. 9 (May 1990) in press.

7. Bruno Nettl, "Thoughts on Improvisation: A Comparative Approach." *The Musical Quarterly* 60, no. 1 (January 1974), 1–19.

8. John Kratus, "A Time Analysis of the Compositional Processes Used by Children Ages 7 to 11." *Journal of Research in Music Education* 37, no.1 (1989), 5–20; Peter Webster, "Creative Thinking in Music: Approaches to Research," in *Music, Society and Education in the United States,* ed. T. Gates (Tuscaloosa, AL: The University of Alabama Press, 1989).

9. Jaques-Dalcroze, *Rhythm, Music and Education,* 75, 76.

10. For musician-educators who pursue Dalcroze certification, however, exercises in piano improvisation are geared toward refining performance skills that are necessary for teaching Eurhythmics.

11. Jaques-Dalcroze, *Rhythm, Music and Education,* 76–79.

PART TWO
Zoltán Kodály

The Kodály Approach

by Beth Landis and Polly Carder

The major goal of Kodály's system of music education was to provide skills in music reading and writing to the entire population of a country. Kodály believed that these skills were essential to the study of all aspects of the art, including its history, analysis, and performance. He believed that everyone in Hungary should receive training in the reading and writing of music just as they received training in the reading and writing of their native language, and that this musical training should come at the same time, during the early years of formal education (see the article "Zoltán Kodály's Legacy to Music Education" by Egon Kraus, reprinted in this book). To carry out this ideal, Kodály instigated a program for public education in music called sol-fa teaching. Primarily a plan for teaching choral musicianship, it stresses the skills of music reading and writing, including sight singing and dictation. It is meant to begin as early as possible in the life of the student and to prepare the student for lifelong enjoyment of music. It is based on acquisition of a vocabulary of rhythmic and melodic motives or patterns.

Like Jaques-Dalcroze, Kodály believed that fundamental knowledge of music is accessible to everyone, not just to a talented few. Both men believed that special methods of teaching could be devised that would bring basic facts and skills of musical communication to their students. Although Kodály knew the work of Jaques-Dalcroze and realized the importance of rhythmic movement as part of musical training, he developed a very different approach. Unlike Jaques-Dalcroze, Kodály saw his program adopted on a nationwide basis in the educational system of his own country.

Kodály gained recognition in three separate but interrelated musical fields. His success in music education was shaped and determined by his achievements as a composer and as a musicologist. As a composer, he is best known for the orchestral suite based on his opera *Háry János*, for *The*

Peacock Variations, and for the *Psalmus hungaricus* for tenor solo, chorus, and orchestra. As a musicologist, he collaborated with Béla Bartók in collecting, classifying, and editing a vast number of Hungarian folk songs. For the schools, he developed a huge repertoire of instructional materials that included his own pedagogical compositions as well as children's choir music. He established the guidelines on which a well-defined curriculum in music education has been built.

> The goals, the philosophy, and the principles were Kodály's. The pedagogy, the means through which to achieve these ends, was not. None of the *practices* associated with Kodály originated with him. Sol-fa was invented in Italy and tonic sol-fa came from England; rhythm syllables were the invention of Emile Chevé in France, and many of the sol-fa techniques employed were taken from the work of Emile Jaques-Dalcroze; hand singing was adapted from the Englishman John Curwen's approach, and the teaching process was basically Pestalozzian.[1]

Kodály believed that music education should begin as early as possible in the life of the individual. Hungarian children often began their musical study in the government's nursery schools, some at the age of $2\frac{1}{2}$ years. At this age, Kodály believed, children are most receptive; their future musical taste is enhanced if they receive the best possible instruction between the ages of three and seven. Kodály believed that the individual child reenacts the musical development of the race, from primitive musical responses to a highly developed level of musicianship. The earliest lessons in music were considered the most important, whether for professional or for amateur musicians of the future, and for beginners, activities and materials were organized in the same way. A carefully planned and systematically developed sequence of musical concepts and experiences is fundamental to the Kodály method of instruction. Rhythmic and melodic concepts, key signatures, meter signatures, and other theoretical symbols are integrated into the study plan at carefully predetermined points. The song material in Kodály's Choral Method series is arranged according to difficulty and offers concentrated practice on each level.

Kodály shared with Orff the belief that with young children, singing and movement are naturally simultaneous. In the nursery school and in the early elementary grades, singing games are an important part of the Kodály plan. Another type of movement appropriate to this method is the traditional patterned folk dance. Early in the study of rhythm and melody, movement is used to reinforce specific ideas. When children are learning about the basic pulse of music, for example, they walk and clap in rhythm with the basic beat. (See the accompanying example.)

(continue walking and clapping throughout)

"No. 17" from Zoltán Kodály, *Pentatonic Music, Volume II,* © Copyright 1958 by Zenemukiado Vallalat, Budapest. Copyright Renewed. English Edition © Copyright 1970 by Boosey & Hawkes Music Publishers, Ltd. Reprinted by permission of Boosey & Hawkes, Inc.

Many of Kodály's 333 *Elementary Exercises* may be sung in connection with basic movements such as walking, running, and marching. The second volume of his *Pentatonic Music* is subtitled *100 Little Marches.* For the most part, it is considered to be the teacher's responsibility to invent appropriate rhythmic movements to accompany songs.

Kodály expressed strong opinions on the formation of musical taste. He felt that an important goal of any music education program is the development of aesthetic sensitivity, and that such development must begin early, since the individual's attitudes toward aesthetic experiences in music will be formed by the time of adolescence. An important part of Hungarian children's education, according to Kodály, was knowledge of their national heritage in music. This meant folk songs as well as the classics of musical literature. Kodály planned an ordered sequence of musical materials for study at all levels, beginning with the nursery school. Some of these materials are available in the United States.

Sol-Fa Teaching

Reading and writing music notation are primary goals in the Kodály system. He considered these skills to be functional and prerequisite to other achievements and learnings. Just as the ability to read and write one's own language is essential to the study of various subjects in the academic curriculum, so in the Kodály philosophy, skill in music reading and writing is essential to all the various aspects of musical study. "Is it imaginable that anybody who is unable to read words can acquire a literary culture or knowledge of any kind? Equally no musical knowledge of any kind can be acquired without the reading of music."[2] Kodály called his method "sol-fa teaching," a name derived from the tonic sol-fa system used in England after about 1840 by John Curwen.

The Curwen system was based on the principle of movable *do* and used syllables to represent pitches. These syllables were abbreviated by their initial letters. Rhythmic values were notated in the Curwen system by punctuation marks. Kodály adopted the initial letters that stood for the syllable names of pitches, but he used other aids for teaching rhythmic notation. Unlike Curwen, Kodály never intended that a system of abbreviated notation should replace the standard staff notation. His plan uses special symbols as aids in teaching pitch and duration only in the early stages of study.

"No. 50" from Zoltán Kodály, *Pentatonic Music, Volume II*, © Copyright 1958 by Zenemukiado Vallalat, Budapest. Copyright Renewed. English Edition © Copyright 1970 by Boosey & Hawkes Music Publishers, Ltd. Reprinted by permission of Boosey & Hawkes, Inc.

Unlike Jaques-Dalcroze and most other European teachers, Kodály used the movable *do* system of solmization, in which syllable names indicate functions within the tonality and relationships among the constituent pitches in a given key, rather than absolute pitch. To distinguish it from the traditional European system of fixed *do*, Kodály called his system "relative sol-fa."

> The essence of *relative solmisation* is that *do* can be on any line or space between the lines. To prevent it getting stuck to one spot, it should be moved about and shown in different positions. It is however the teacher's job not to overdo this. If he sees that the children are experiencing difficulty over the moving of the *do*, he must keep it in the same place for a time; during a whole lesson, or several lessons if necessary. Should however *do* become fixed rigidly to the same spot, it will be very difficult to move it to another position, even within the range of the same clef.
>
> The ability to shift from one tonic to another is the secret of good reading. This is facilitated by using sol-fa syllables, and should be developed slowly and consistently.[3]

Relative sol-fa teaching is a well-developed, sequential plan based on acquisition of a vocabulary of rhythmic and melodic motives or patterns. These patterns are analogous to the words and phrases that make up initial learning experiences in language. The child encounters rhythmic and melodic motives first through singing and hearing them. They are abstracted from the musical context and repeated many times. The child comes to recognize them first as sounds, then in other forms of concrete and spatial representation. These representations might include colored sticks or children standing alone and with linked arms (| | ⊓ |) to express rhythmic motives; big body motion describing the melody line, later transcribed to hand signals and eventually reduced to staff notation. Only after a child is thoroughly familiar with rhythmic and melodic patterns through a variety of experiences is the transference to staff notation consciously learned. In this way the earliest experiences with notation, like the reading of language, represent ideas the child is already using. The repertoire of musical patterns is used in establishing interrelationships among the constituent tones of a key, in elementary sightsinging and in creative ways. The following syllable names and abbreviations are used in the Kodály system:

do	re	mi	fa	so	la	ti	do
d	r	m	f	s	l	t	d'

After the syllable *ti* in the ascending order of the scale tones, the next or eighth tone in the series (*do*) is marked with an apostrophe. When tones above this high *do* are used, they are similarly marked. Tones below the key tone in a descending order, (*ti, la,* and *so,* for example) are identified by commas: *so, la, ti, do re mi fa so la ti do' re' mi'.* Note that, while the syllable *sol* is normally used in the United States, Hungarian children normally sing *so. So* may be easier to use than *sol,* especially when followed by the syllable *la.* Early in their musical study children use these syllables in singing at different pitch levels, so that the idea of movable *do* becomes a practical reality to them. Syllable names and functions of pitches are introduced in a definite order that is strictly followed. Beginning with the so-called universal chant of childhood, the descending minor third or *so–mi,* pitches are introduced one at a time.

so	mi			
la	so	mi		
la	so	mi	do	
la	so	mi	re	do
fa				
ti[4]				

There is much reinforcement of the scale tones, even when so few are involved: Kodály wrote dozens of exercises restricted to a range of two, three, four, or five tones. In the following exercise, *do* is on G.

"No. 29" from Zoltán Kodály, *333 Elementary Exercises*, © Copyright 1962 by Zoltán Kodály. English Edition © Copyright 1964 by Boosey & Hawkes Music Publishers, Ltd. Revised English Edition © Copyright 1970 by Boosey & Hawkes Music Publishers, Ltd. Reprinted by permission of Boosey & Hawkes, Inc.

In contrast with systems that introduce all eight tones of the major scale early in the learning sequence, this system adds *la* and *so* below the tonal center to the repertoire of pitches before completing the major scale within an octave.

"No. 47" from Zoltán Kodály, *Fifty Nursery Songs*, © Copyright 1954 by Zenemukiado Vallalat, Budapest; Copyright Renewed. English Edition © Copyright 1962 by Boosey & Co. Ltd. Revised English Edition © Copyright 1968 by Boosey & Co. Ltd. Reprinted by permission of Boosey & Hawkes, Inc.

When students have acquired full use of the diatonic range and the chromatic syllables *fi, si,* and *ta,* they may also use the sol-fa syllables to learn the principles of modulation(see "No.3," *Tricinia*).

Many examples of songs built on the limited number of pitches used with beginning students are found in Hungarian folk music. However, it was because Kodály could not find enough songs with small range and simple rhythms that he wrote his *Fifty Nursery Songs.* He often expressed surprise that other countries wished to adapt his method, and his first advice to teachers in foreign countries was to identify a large body of folk material of their own country. Kodály considered *fa* and *ti* hardest of the diatonic scale degrees to sing in tune, particularly for children. Without careful training and extensive practice, people tend to sing *fa* slightly sharp and *ti* slightly flat.

This does not mean, however, that songs with these scale tones are eliminated from the students' repertoire.

"No. 3" from Zoltán Kodály, *Tricinia*, © Copyright 1954 by Zenemukiado Vallalat, Budapest; Copyright renewed. English Edition © Copyright 1964 by Boosey & Hawkes Music Publishers, Ltd. Reprinted by Permission of Boosey & Hawkes, Inc.

Some songs with *fa* and *ti* must be taught, and there should, as well, be a few songs with notes beyond the most comfortable singing range of the children. If children cannot say the letter R correctly ("See the wabbit wun!") parents do not eliminate all Rs from their own speech. Instead, they pronounce Rs carefully, distinctly, and correctly. They provide a model for learning: "See the *r*abbit *r*un!" So it is with singing. While most songs should be within the comfortable tessitura of young singers, some songs must include the difficult-to-sing minor seconds, and some must extend the range a bit. Only if these sounds exist in the children's experience will they ever acquire them.[5]

Fa and *ti* were introduced in the first volume of Kodály's *Bicinia Hungarica*. He suggested that, to prepare students for reading them, special two-part intonation exercises be sung. These exercises stress the relationship of *fa* and *ti* with neighboring scale tones.

The basic mode of instruction in Kodály's method is singing. He believed that the voice is the most immediate and personal way of expressing oneself in music, and he realized that in many Hungarian schools, instruments of various kinds would be unavailable. By means of vocal music the ear could best be trained to distinguish intervals and to keep the young musicians in tune. As in the Dalcroze method, such training as this preceded instrumental study. He expected it to enhance the enjoyment of adults participating in choral groups and attending concerts. One of the basic ideas underlying the Kodály method is that singing should be done in an especially careful way—that students should be taught to use their voices as well as possible, with pure tone and accurate intonation. Development of inner hearing contributes to this ideal, as does the fact that children gain a great deal of experience in singing.

"No. 35" from Zoltán Kodály, *66 Two-Part Exercies,* © Copyright 1963 by Zenemukiado Vallalat, Budapest. English Edition © Copyright 1964 by Boosey and Hawkes Music Publishers, Ltd. Reprinted by permission of Boosey and Hawkes, Inc.

Kodály believed that voices are best accompanied by other voices rather than by instruments. In this way the singer learns the skills of choral singing, such as blending his or her voice with other voices, maintaining his or her part independently of other singers, and most important in Kodály's opinion, singing in tune. Children imitate the teacher's example in learning about melody and phrasing. The teacher also sings musical examples in which children listen for various other musical elements. Correct intonation is developed through exercises like the ones in *Let Us Sing Correctly* in which all tones are of long duration, so that singers may tune their voices with others. In the earliest exercises one part moves while the other remains constant. These exercises are meant to be sung initially from hand signs given by the teacher; later the same exercises may be read from the book.

Part singing is first introduced through easy canons and melodic ostinatos. One of the ways to achieve independence in part singing is through exercises using canonic imitation, as in *Sixty-Six Two-Part Exercises* and *Fifteen Two-Part Exercises*. Skill in sightsinging is developed progressively through Kodály's *Seventy-Seven, Sixty-Six, Fifty-Five, Forty-Four, Thirty-Three,* and *Twenty-Two Two-Part Exercises*, the last being the most difficult and not really intended for children's classes. The four volumes of *Bicinia Hungarica* contain 108 selections for two-part singing. While the musical and pedagogical value of these pieces is unquestionable, their use outside the country of their origin is limited because of the essentially Hungarian character of the melodies. Early followers of the Kodály method in the United States saw the need for collections of indigenous American songs that would meet the needs of their classes, and gradually more collections of appropriate songs are becoming available. Among the techniques for strengthening part singing and inner hearing are several in which singers exchange parts at a signal from the teacher. This practice is begun in the elementary school years (see "No.3," *Bicinia Hungarica, Volume I*).

Through a process called automatic recognition, children build a vocabulary of rhythmic and melodic patterns. These patterns are sung, written, practiced in hand signs, represented in movement, and used in improvisation. Specific musical motives are recognized by the child as are words or phrases used many times in spoken language: first in isolation and then in a musical context. Children may observe similarities and dissimilarities among motives, find familiar patterns in new songs, and analyze the starting motives of songs and group together all the songs that begin with the same melodic pattern.

Automatically-recognized motives of music become part of the "activity repertoire" of the child; he recalls, recognizes, sings, sounds, makes hand signals. Motives appear in new situations all the time and are fixed in their so-fa and rhythmical form.

If the child has good ability to read from notes he will do it not through outer direction but by a sort of inner compulsion on the basis of his former knowledge.... *The child owns a rich inner repertoire of motives and he chooses from them* when writing down a new rhythm or melody, or when reading aloud an unknown song.[6]

"No. 3" from Zoltán Kodály, *Bicinia Hungarica*, Volume I, © Copyright 1942 by Zoltán Kodály; Copyright Renewed. English Edition © Copyright 1962 by Boosey & Co. Ltd. Revised English Edition © Copyright 1968 by Boosey & Co. Ltd. Reprinted by permission of Boosey & Hawkes, Inc.

There is a great deal of practice on the children's vocabulary of melodic patterns. The melodic interval *so–mi* (5–3), for example, is isolated and recognized in as many familiar songs as possible. Children sing questions and answers on the two tones:

Where is El- len? Here I am.
  s   s   m   m   s   s   m

Hand Signal Chart

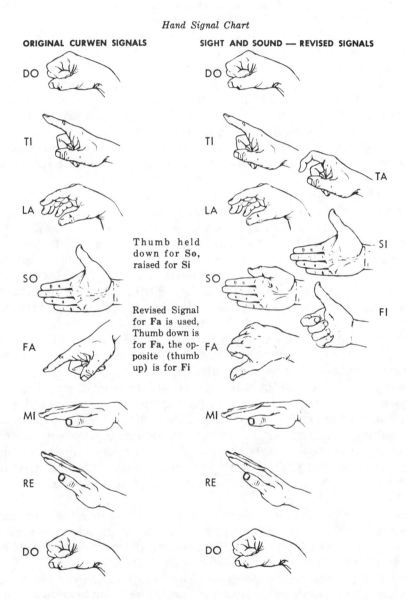

"Hand Signal Chart" from Arpad Darazs and Stephen Jay, *Sight and Sound* © Copyright 1965 by Boosey & Hawkes, Inc. Reprinted by permission.

Pictorial representations are used, with and without the musical staff, in discussing which tone is higher and which lower. Body movements and hand signs reinforce the pitch relationship.

One of the distinguishing characteristics of the Kodály system is the use of hand signs to represent melodic interrelationships. In the nineteenth century, hand signs were associated with the tonic sol-fa method of John Curwen. They utilize the pull of certain scale tones toward the tonal center and toward the fairly stationary sounds of *mi* and *so*; *ti*, represented by pointing upward, tends toward *do*; *fa*, with the thumb pointing downward, tends toward *mi*; *re*, with the hand pointing obliquely upward, also tends toward *mi*. Hand signs are used to teach interval relationships. The teacher introduces hand signs, like the sounds they represent, in a strict order, beginning with *so–mi* and continuing with the presentation of one syllable at a time. Small children often make these signs with both hands simultaneously.

The child's experiences reinforce each other and eventually lead to automatic recognition of rhythmic, as well as melodic, sounds and symbols. In the study of quarter rests, for example, as the student listens to a song or exercise, he or she discovers a silence in the music that has the duration of a quarter note. As the student sings in imitation of the teacher, he or she produces the same silence within the music. The student claps the rhythm of the song or exercise and observes the rest with appropriate silence. Later there will be other games involving clapping or tapping that will reinforce the concept the student is formulating. Pictorial representations are used in Hungarian textbooks to show durations of tones as well as rests. The size and the grouping of pictures can be used to illustrate rhythmic ideas found in certain songs.

Rhythm patterns, like melody patterns, are introduced according to a carefully ordered sequence of difficulty, through the medium of folk song material. "The broad outlines of the Kodály sequence are designed to suit the maturity levels of the child; the small sequences within the overall sequence are based upon the frequency of occurrence of a particular rhythmic figure or melodic turn in the song material being used for teaching—the folk songs and art music from which new learnings are to be drawn."[7]

Beat is introduced first. Note values are learned through the experience of singing and hearing them, isolating them in songs, and representing them by means of the time names, by notation, and by stems without note heads. Rhythm patterns are reinforced in several ways, especially in pictorial representation, respondent games, and body movement. Stems and flags alone, without note heads, are used to represent quarter-note and eighth-note values when first introduced. In the materials Kodály prepared, standard notes and rests are used, but often without the staff. Hungarian teachers have frequently presented rhythmic stems without noteheads in the classroom before teaching conventional rhythmic notation. Hungarian elementary school textbooks have sometimes used stems and flags alone.

> Initially one should devise some simple pictorial representation of the rhythm elements which correspond with the single down stroke of the crotchet (quarter-note) and the two down strokes joined by a ligature for the pair of quavers (eighth notes). A good example, taken from an early text book by Kodály and Professor Adam, is to use pictures of boots: large boots for the slower steps of father, and pairs of small boots to represent the faster steps of the child who takes two steps to every one stride of his father. Once this idea has become established in the child's mind, pictorial representation can give way to conventional rhythm symbols.[8]

Helga Szabo, an authority on the Kodály method, presented an interesting way of teaching children to recall rhythm patterns. From Kodály's *Pentatonic Music* (volume III), children sang exercises in sol-fa; other children responded by clapping the rhythms of these exercises from memory.[9] Children acquire their first practice in writing melodic notation by placing note heads on a large staff. In preparation for writing rhythms, they use sticks to represent Kodály's staffless rhythmic notation.

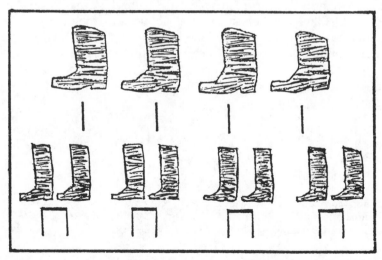

From Helga Szabo, *The Kodaly Concept of Music Education*, English edition by Geoffrey Russell-Smith (London: Boosey & Hawkes Music Publishers Ltd., 1969), 9. Used by permission of Boosey & Hawkes, Inc.

The expanding vocabulary of patterns in rhythm and melody is used as a basis for several learning procedures other than reading and writing notation. Creative activities in the Kodály system are centered around the patterns or motives children know. Games, songs, and exercises are improvised with these musical microstructures as material. Definite plans and goals are kept in mind during improvisation; aimless exploration of sounds is not encouraged. Children analyze the music that other members of their class have improvised.

Many ear-training exercises are directed toward development of a skill called "inner hearing." Children learn to recognize intervals, to distinguish interrelationships among scale tones, and to sing whole songs or exercises silently. These exercises begin in kindergarten, when children interrupt their singing at a signal from the teacher to sing silently until the next signal indicates that they are to sing aloud again. Silent singing is used also when children begin learning to sing in parts. To develop inner hearing, children may read a short song or exercise silently from the chalkboard. After they have memorized it, the music is erased and they sing it aloud.

Kodály recommended that the first instrument children use should be a xylophone with removable bars. Beginning with two bars for playing *so–mi*, the teacher and class add other bars as the corresponding scale degrees are introduced. Children encounter the recorder as their second instrument. In playing it, children learn the letter names of absolute pitches and corresponding names of lines and spaces on the treble staff. The study of piano is deferred until students have a good background in vocal music, ideally until they can prehear musical notation as they read it. Kodály recommended that the study of piano begin with the black keys, and that two-part canons be used to develop independence of the hands. He suggested that two-part canons best illustrate the principle of polyphony when the pianist plays both parts by reading from a single line of notation.[10]

"No. 1" from Zoltán Kodály, Twenty Four Little Canons on the Black Keys. © Copyright 1954 by Zenemukiado Vallalat, Budapest. © Copyright assigned 1957 to Boosey & Co. Ltd. Copyright renewd. Reprinted by permission of Boosey & Hawkes, Inc.

Teachers working within the Kodály approach make extensive plans, often covering a year's work for each grade. In addition to these general plans naming the skills and concepts to be taught in each grade, the teacher makes detailed plans for each lesson, listing the materials and the instructional procedures to be used. Long-range goals and immediate goals are reviewed regularly. A typical lesson includes familiarization with songs containing rhythmic and melodic patterns to be taught later, concentration on songs containing the patterns on which today's lesson focuses, and review of songs containing patterns previously learned.

The Instructional Repertoire

Kodály believed that only the best musical literature should be used in the instructional repertoire. Children, he thought, are particularly sensitive to works of art, and should experience only serious compositions of a high quality. According to Kodály's philosophy, contemporary composers should write serious children's music in the smaller forms needed for teaching materials, but felt that not every gifted composer is suited to writing music for children. He stated that the main prerequisite for such a composer is to have the soul and spirit of a child. Songs contrived according to an adult's concept of childhood tastes and understandings should be eliminated. He considered commercial popular songs and even songs from operettas and Broadway shows to be of doubtful pedagogical value. He believed that music of an inferior quality is actually harmful to the development of musical taste, and dwelling on such music in childhood can handicap later appreciation and enjoyment of better music.

Attitudes and behaviors shaped in the early years, he thought, are influenced by music used in teaching. Teaching with low-quality instructional materials can result in poorer quality musical experiences—not only during a vital period of concept formation, but in later life as well. "Kodály's premise is that the small child learns first through singing games, next through the folk songs of his own region and country, then through international folk song which is a bridge to art form and the classics of composed music."[11] Singing games are used in nursery and kindergarten classes because they are a natural activity of childhood, combining movement with music. They are a part of the child's cultural heritage, traditional songs with patterned movements that are inseparable from the songs themselves.

There are two stages in the learning of folk songs. First, the student learns a considerable number of folk songs of his own country, even of his own region, and then his repertoire is extended to include the folk music of other peoples (see article "Folk Song in Pedagogy" by Zoltán Kodály reprinted in this book). Folk music has been called a natural subject matter for teaching. Several reasons for this are given by the Hungarian teachers implementing the Kodály method and by their American counterparts teaching in this country. Folk music can be considered part of the culture indigenous to a particular people, expressing shared thoughts and feelings that symbolize a kind of unity within the nation and with the past. The folk songs of their own country provide Hungarian children with, in the words of several outstanding Hungarian teachers, a "musical mother tongue." According to Kodály, this is true for children of every culture.

Farmer Jacob
Folk-song

Sol-fa indications have been omitted from this piece to provide an opportunity for the young singers to find the 'doh' for themselves.

Folk music may be considered closest to the life experiences of rural children and to the cultural heritage of urban ones. This music is a virtually limitless source of the musical motives and patterns that are essential in the

Kodály plan. Many folk songs are in the pentatonic mode, and Kodály, like Orff, considered this mode to be the easiest and most natural for children to learn in their early lessons. There is a close relationship in these songs between music and language.

> The singing of folksongs must form a part of every music lesson; not only to provide practice in them for their own sake, but to maintain continuity and to awaken, develop and maintain the sense of relationship between music and the language. For there is no denying that it is here, in folksong, that the most perfect relationship between music and language can be found.[12]

Folk songs of other lands are added next to the student's repertoire.

Kodály had definite purposes in mind when he compiled the various books in his instructional series. The four volumes of *Pentatonic Music* supplemented available folk song material. Volume one of *Pentatonic Music* contains one hundred Hungarian folk songs notated in sol-fa initials and notes without a staff. Volume two is used at the kindergarten level to establish the feeling for pulse through marching, walking, or clapping the beat. Melodies in this volume are considered simple enough for the youngest school child. To implement his idea that scale tones should be introduced gradually and practiced a great deal, Kodály grouped together nineteen studies using the two tones *do* and *re* at the beginning of the *333 Elementary Exercises*. The next thirty-six exercises in the book are built on three tones: eleven exercises on *do–la–so*, seventeen on *re–do–la*, and eight on *mi–re–do*.

Some of the materials Kodály wrote were intended to be used in a cyclical way. The *50 Nursery Songs,* for example, are learned in kindergarten by rote. Children in the primary grades read the same songs from the book. A few of these songs are reprinted in *333 Elementary Exercises* for the same purpose.

Historical Development

The Kodály method of music education originated under conditions that were favorable to the goal of teaching all children to read and write music. In state-controlled schools with a long heritage of strict academic training in the European style, it was possible to establish in Hungary a structured curriculum for vocal music classes on a nationwide scale. Goals for music education were established by the state. Instructional materials were specified, and standards of achievement were defined for each grade level, from the nursery school through the institutions that train teachers. For most children, classes in vocal music meeting twice a week for forty-five minutes were a requirement through the eighth grade. In the last two years of public school, choral training was emphasized. Instrumental study was not encouraged until children could read and write music at a certain level, and was not generally considered a part of the course offerings for everyone. Teachers of this method felt that "until children can prehear the note they are going to produce, they cannot produce that note in tune except on a keyboard."[13]

In Hungary, there were Music Primary Schools in which the study of vocal music was more intensive than in the other primary and elementary schools. Children were selected on the basis of musical tests. About 130 Music Primary Schools were established between 1950 and 1970.

> In 1950 the first singing primary school was established in Kesckemet, Kodály's birthplace, under the direction of his longtime friend, the school principal Marta Nemesszeghy. Here children received music instruction every day of the school week, and the method was further developed and refined. As a result of the phenomenal success of Nemesszeghy and the children at the Kesckemet school, the next years saw a rapid rise in the development and dissemination of this method, from the nursery school level to the conservatories and the most advanced classes of the Franz Liszt Academy of Music in Budapest.[14]

Instructional principles and procedures that were developed for a country roughly the size of Indiana spread to many countries. At the 1958 conference of the International Society for Music Education, Jeno Adam introduced the Kodály method. At successive meetings of the conference in

1961 and 1963, other Hungarian specialists lectured on it, and in 1964 Kodály addressed the conference, which that year was held in Budapest. Teachers from several nations visited Hungary, and many of them spoke with Kodály in person. In these ways the ideas basic to his method were carried to the Soviet Union, Czechoslovakia, Denmark, Finland, France, West Germany, Belgium, Argentina, Chile, Peru, Switzerland, Canada, Japan, and Australia. Like the ideas of Jaques-Dalcroze and Orff, the principles of the Kodály method were brought to the United States by Europeans now living in this country and by Americans who went to Europe to study.

Jeno Adam worked closely with Kodály, and it was Adam who first presented the method in writing. The original pedagogical sequence was a result of Adam's work. His manual for Hungarian teachers was translated into English by Louis Boros and others. The Boros translation contained a detailed, explicit plan for teaching music reading, the writing of rhythmic and melodic notation, and ear training. It included 113 songs adapted from Hungarian folklore. The instructional plan used sol-fa syllables and their initial letters, stem notation to indicate rhythmic values, hand signs, rhythm names such as *ta* and *ti-ti*, and a symbol called the movable *do* clef that indicates the position of *do* on the staff.

Alexander Ringer initiated an early experimental program in New Haven, Connecticut, to apply Kodály principles and practices in American schools. Denise Bacon organized summer courses and presented some of the leading Hungarian music educators as teachers and lecturers. Following her study in Hungary (1967–68) she opened a training institute in September 1969. Its program was developed with the help and support of Mrs. Zoltán Kodály, Marta Nemesszeghy, and the Hungarian Minister of Education. Since that time, several other centers of study for Kodály education have developed in the United States. Among them are Holy Names College in Oakland, California, The Kodály Musical Training Institute in West Hartford, Connecticut, and Silver Lake College in Manitowac, Wisconsin.

The Organization of American Kodály Educators holds annual national conferences and publishes a periodical, The *Kodály Envoy*, with news of the society and its chapters, notices of workshops and new publications, articles on topics for the classroom, and scholarly articles on such topics as "Syllable Systems—Kodály's Choices." The organization can be contacted at 131 Second Street, Framingham, MA 01701. The International Kodály Society, founded in 1973 and based in Budapest, is an honorary society made up of outstanding teachers of the Kodály method.

The study of folk songs was vital to Kodály's plan for music education. In each of the countries that has adopted Kodály's principles, educators have made efforts to gather and classify the folk music of that country for use in place of the Hungarian songs. Kodály believed that every nationality has a wealth of folk music that can be used to teach basic elements of musical structure, and he said the United States has the richest possibility of all, because of its diversified ethnic groups. He noted that "The life of folk music changes from country to country and from time to time. Other nations cannot follow the peculiar road of Hungarian development."[15] He suggested that the 40,000 folk songs in the Library of Congress Archive of American Folk Song be used as a major resource. Extensive collections of songs have been built in the major centers of Kodály training, where a great many songs have been analyzed and classified according to the rhythmic and melodic patterns they contain.

Notes

1. Lois Chosky, Robert Abrahmson, Avon Gillespie, and David Woods, *Teaching Music in the Twentieth Century* (Englewood Cliffs, NJ: Prentice Hall, 1986), 70.

2. Zoltán Kodály, *Visszatekintes* (published by Zenemukiado, 1964). Quoted in Helga Szabo, *The Kodaly Concept of Music Education:* English edition by Geoffry Russell-Smith (London: Boosey and Hawkes, 1969), 10.

3. Kodály, *Visszatekintes*, 13.

4. Helga Szabo, *The Kodaly Concept of Music Education*. Textbook with three records; English edition by Geoffrey Russell-Smith (London: Boosey and Hawkes, 1969).

5. Lois Choksy, *The Kodály Method: Comprehensive Music Education from Infant to Adult*, 2d ed. (Englewood Cliffs, NJ: Prentice Hall, 1988), 33.

6. Klara Kokas, "The Transfer Effect of the Kodaly Method of Music Education." Lecture delivered at the Teacher Training Workshop, Dana School of Music, Wellesley, MA, August 8, 1969.

7. Lois Choksy et al., 78.

8. Szabo, *The Kodály Concept*, 9.

9. Szabo, *The Kodály Concept*, record album.

10. Szabo, *The Kodaly Concept*, 20.

11. Denise Bacon, "Can the Kodaly Method Be Successfully Adapted Here?" *Musart* 22, No. 5 (April–May 1970), 14.

12. Kodaly, *Visszatekintes*, 13.

13. Geoffry Russell-Smith, "Introducing Kodaly Principles into Elementary Teaching," *Music Educators Journal* 54, No. 3 (November 1967), 44.

14. Russell-Smith, 44.

15. Vikar.

Folk Song in Pedagogy

by Zoltán Kodály

The Hungarian people have provided one of the best examples of how to use folk songs for educational purposes. The natural life of village people, flourishing as it did up to the First World War, was always accompanied by music and dance. Little children as soon as they began to speak, or even before, warbled ditties which they learned, however inaccurately, from their seniors. As they grew they gradually acquired all songs suitable to their age. In church they joined the community, learned the hymns by ear and, before adulthood, collected a substantial repertoire of songs. All children practiced dancing; their games began with dance-rounds. One could have observed adult people teaching the secrets of man's dancing to five-year old boys.

In more recent times, with the growth of towns and cities, children were deprived of the natural musical spontaneity that flourished in the villages. Nor was the kindergarten able to provide the musical orientation found in natural village life. Today, as the old-style life undergoes radical changes and even villages have kindergartens, these schools must perpetuate musical traditions if they are to survive.

Obviously, all reasonable pedagogy has to start from the first spontaneous utterances of the child, rhythmic-melodic expressions with repeated simple phrases which slowly give way to more complex structures. Since children learn most easily between the ages of three and six, the kindergartens would be able to accomplish much more in music if they would observe this pedagogic principle.

The fortunate child who can take part in singing games, whether in kindergarten or in free play with other children, has a great advantage over those who never had an opportunity to do so. The elementary school should carefully examine whether or not the child has had this advantage. If not, the school has the duty to provide it, for without this foundation, no further progress is possible. Thus elementary schools first have to recapitulate the material of the kindergarten, such as singing games and rhythmical plays connected with physical movements, preferably in close cooperation with physical training. This foundation may vary with different peoples, although if one runs through the first volume of *Corpus Musicae Popularis Hungaricae*,[1] containing children's games, he will find many international motives which verify the unity of mankind. However, since the singing games of every country are strongly dependent on their respective languages, even they are colored with nationalistic tradition.

The next step would be the folk song. Each nation has a rich variety of folk songs suitable for teaching purposes; if selected in a graded order, they furnish the best material to introduce musical elements so that the student will be conscious of them. Surprisingly quick results can be obtained by having the student sing by ear, then take dictation from the teacher. It is essential that the material used should be musically attractive. In some countries that still use the unpopular, dry, and lifeless exercises, the children grow to hate the music lesson. Incidentally, at least two lessons weekly are imperative. No result is to be hoped for if the children do not await the music lesson with thrilled expectation. If they do not feel refreshed by an exciting lesson, all labor is lost.

In Hungary, singing in elementary schools has been compulsory since 1868. Even so, as a consequence of bad teaching, many people have finished school with a hatred of music. Only the last few decades have improved the teacher's training so that tolerable results can be obtained, even with two weekly lessons. After 1945, we were able to initiate experimental schools with daily singing lessons. The results were surprising and convincing. The surplus of four hours is not an overburden; on the contrary, the progress in every other subject became easier and quicker. I dare say we may attribute this result mostly to the folk song, which is our chief material. Folk songs offer such a rich variety of moods and perspectives, that the child grows in human consciousness, and feels more and more at home in his country.

After exhausting the national treasure of rhythm and melody, foreign folk songs are the best way to introduce other types of music. As in the teaching of languages, the beginning must be unilingual. Afterwards, it should be enlarged, first by neighboring or related music and later by music of more distant peoples. Thus we are by no means chauvinistically limited to the Hungarian folk song. To become international we first have to belong to one distinct people and to speak its language properly, not in gibberish. To understand other people, we must first understand ourselves. And nothing will accomplish this better than a thorough knowledge of one's native folk songs. Later, he may proceed to comprehend other people through their folk songs.

The final purpose of all this must be to instill in the pupils the understanding and love of the great classics of the past. These are much nearer to the folk song than is generally recognized, for direct expression and clear form are common in folk songs. Haydn, the best master with whom to begin, has salient connection with folk songs. Even in many works of Mozart there is the sublimated Austrian folk song which is easy to recognize. Beethoven, as well, wrote many themes that were folklike.

The playing of instruments facilitates much musical learning in the higher grades, but singing must always be in the center. In our musical elementary schools, instruments are not compulsory, but many children want to play an instrument, and follow the advice of their teachers in choosing a suitable one. In those schools, our purpose is not so much the training of instrumental soloists, as it is the preparation of students for participation in chamber and orchestral music. Some of the larger schools are able to perform concerti of Vivaldi or other works of similar difficulty. The nonplaying pupils are the performing students' understanding and thankful audience, and once grown up, they will be the best audience for great music. In this way they fulfill the purpose of those schools and of all our endeavors.

The pedagogical approach used by Leonard Bernstein in his television programs, also published in book form with records, is most interesting and witty, but is by no means a satisfying way to educate a truly expert public.[2] This is a most crucial problem, and in every country one can notice the disproportion between the performing artist and his audience. Though attempts to educate a music-loving and musically knowledgeable public are numerous, their success is dependent upon developing an audience of active listeners.

This is the goal to be reached in our schools, but music educators give their pupils much more. As they make students better musicians, they also make them better human beings. There is a German saying that a bad musician may be a fairly good man, but a good musician is, *ceteris paribus* (all other things being equal), a better man. The good musician certainly is more balanced, many-sided, and equally developed bodily and mentally. The introduction of a music program that perpetuates tradition and provides a solid musical foundation into the curriculum of general education would greatly enrich the human race.

Notes

1. G. Kerényi, ed., *Gyermekjátékok* [Children's Games]. Volume 1 of *Corpus musicae popularis Hungaricae*, ed. Béla Bartók and Zoltán Kodály (Budapest: Hungarian Academy of Sciences, 1951).

2. Leonard Bernstein, *Young People's Concerts for Reading and Listening* (1962; rev. ed. New York: N.p. 1970).

Egon Kraus has been the secretary-general of the national music education organization in Germany and both general secretary and president of the International Society of Music Education, and was a close friend and colleague of Kodály. This article appeared in the fall 1967 issue of the *International Music Educator*.

Zoltán Kodály's Legacy to Music Education

by Egon Kraus

Kodály published thirty-three studies and essays, which in their entirety present a complete picture of a unified concept of music education. Basic questions concerning musical education are so treated that an organic structure is recognizable in which the general and professional musical education is seen as a common entity. Through all these essays the battle against musical illiteracy runs like a red thread as a prerequisite for the erection of an independent musical culture.

Music in the Kindergarten

The musical education of children cannot begin early enough. In Kodály's essay "Music in the Kindergarten" (1941-1958) one can read: "In the Kindergarten the child learns while playing. It is already too late to do this in the elementary school. The new psychology states emphatically that the age from three to seven years is much more important for education than the later years. What is spoiled or missed in these years can never be repaired or recovered again later. In these years the fate of the man is decided for his lifetime. If the soul lies fallow until the seventh year it will also be unreceptive to later sowing."

Song and play belong together for the child. "The simple song does not hinder the action of play, rather the opposite; it makes play more attractive,

79

more interesting. The limited time available for musical education of the child can thus be extended on the playground without diminishing the time for other activities. The instinctive, natural speech of the child is song, and the younger the child, the more he desires to express himself in movement."

Kodály laid the blame for the unmusical or even hostile attitude of the Hungarian society toward music on the failure of the former kindergartens and primary schools. His criticism was turned especially toward the song literature which he felt was "neither satisfactory for the national nor the general humanistic education. The poor quality of melody did not lead the children to good music but rather to musical trash. It did not develop the musical possibilities as far as the child's talents would allow."

Above all Kodály scolds those educators who think that "a watered-down substitute of art is good enough to serve as learning material. Only the best is just good enough for children. Everything else is only damaging. No one is too great to write for children. Quite the opposite—one should strive to be worthy of this task. What is needed are original works which in text, in melody, and in atmosphere take cognizance of the child spirit and voice."

Still in 1957, Kodály complained about the continued use of the piano in accompanying children's song and play, their rhythmic-musical exercises and even the telling of fairy tales. "When the child becomes used to seeking only and continuously for the extra-musical illustration in music he will never understand music. When a song is always accompanied the feeling for the beauty of the pure melodic line is destroyed and it is just this which should be cultivated as the primary goal."

The kindergarten age can be used throughout for playful and child-suitable work with musical elements. For such work, melodies with simple rhythms in the pentatonic area are most suitable. Such melodies should be sung by the children without texts and finally with tonic sol-fa syllables. "The ear training of children develops faster if the songs are learned through their melodic line rather than from the text."

Kindergarten and primary school teachers are usually opposed to solmization because they themselves do not have command of this simple system. The syllables are fun for the child, and he masters the basis of musical thinking in a playful way through their use. "Actually there is no difficulty in teaching six to seven year old children sol-fa singing. If they enter school with the knowledge of sol-fa singing the singing instruction would progress much faster."

Kodály never gets tired of praising the advantages of the pentatonic scale for music education in kindergarten and primary grade. "There are still too many kindergarten teachers and others who plague little ones with songs set in a large range and continuing large intervals, and thereby endanger the musical and vocal development of the child. A child who is too early pressured into the use of diatonic melodies will never learn to sing accurately in tune. A good ear will always detect the deviations between mi and fa (the teacher who always sings loudly with the children naturally will not hear this even if she, by chance, sings with perfect intonation). If, however, the children have gained security in the use of the five principal tones of the pentatonic the use and aural arrangement of the half steps will cause no difficulty."

At another time Kodály states, "tonal consciousness and the capability to sing tones correctly develops better with the use of pentatonic melodies which mix tonal steps and leaps, than with the diatonic tonal `ladder-climbing'."

The pentatonic sharpens the ear, captures the attention, and encourages tune perfection in singing. Pentatonic melodies contain characteristic motives which make stronger impressions since they function as units and are perceived as such.

Conditions are similar in the area of rhythm. Kodály begins with simple rhythms, but these are from the very beginning characteristic and dynamic. Rhythmic life makes the perception, recognition, and memory of melodies much easier.

In place of piano accompaniment Kodály suggests childlike percussion and barred instruments. The melody instruments (for example the cymbalon-psalter) should be pentatonically tuned. Every child would be able to learn the use of these instruments very early. "In this way the invaluable possibilities to do something for the musical education of the child, and at the same time to satisfy his compulsion to act, are made available."

Music in the School

The basis of school music education is the development and cultivation of the human voice. The music instruction in the elementary school is primarily singing instruction. "A thorough musical education is only possible where singing has been the basis. The playing of an instrument is often only possible for a few selected individuals. Only the human voice, which is a possession of everyone, and at the same time the most beautiful of all instruments, can serve as the basis for a general musical culture."

The child must learn to read notes through song before he holds an instrument in his hands. "Lucky the child who receives his first associations with notation through his own singing. When he begins to sing and, at the same time, is burdened with the notions of instrument techniques he will no longer be able to recognize the vocal ideas as primary or fundamental. If he never sings at all he will achieve a free and inner music making only with great difficulty, if at all. The disadvantages of an education which is not built on song cannot be overcome even by the greatest musical gift."

Kodály decided in favor of the relative sol-fa syllables at a very early date. Besides many other didactic considerations the most important factor in this decision was the one that the pupils would gain command over their voices through systematic solfège instruction. The goal of this instruction is that the aural and the visual picture of music should make an indivisible unit. The relative sol-fa method clarifies the relationship of tones between one another, the tonal relegations being easily realized and understood especially if strengthened by the use of hand signs.

The systematic solfège instruction begins in primary school and must be continued through the highest classes of singing and instrumental playing, "until one can read notes as an educated adult reads a book; silently, but with the most exact and actual idea of its sound.... One who does not hear what he sees, and who cannot see what he hears, does not deserve to be called a musician."

Kodály feels that the failure of music education up to now is due to the fact that no suitable method of elementary music education has been used. "A mechanical instrumental instruction, making music with fingers only, not with the spirit, the neglect of musical basic instruction, solfège, is the direct cause of the decline of singing and also the increase of second class professional musicians and dilettantes who overestimate their own capacities."

Music education must be built on one's own musical tradition. The musical mother tongue is the foundation of musical instruction. "Our musical education process during the last seventy years was a mistake, and therefore it remained without success. One wanted to educate the people to music by discarding all that which the people knew for themselves. But one can build only on something that is already at hand. If we do not build on our own musical tradition then we build on sand."

The folksong is not the song of uneducated classes but rather the inheritance of the people. "It is not a primitive form, but rather the matured, clarified art resulting from centuries of development. It is the most complete expression of the national soul, the nucleus and basic stock of national musical culture. The shortest way to the folksong is by way of musical education." Obviously an organically planned music education must go beyond the folksong. "But in order to do this we must encompass the folksong."

Only when one's own musical tradition has become again the national source and basis of all musical education the way to the music of the world opens itself more and more. "We are closer to the realization of a world music than of a world literature that Goethe imagined. But the question is, how can we take our place in world music more quickly; through loosing or strengthening our individuality? Perhaps one would think that we would be better musical world-citizens the more we cultivated a world outlook and the more we neglected our own, but I believe just the opposite. The more we cultivate and study our own music the more we shall be able to contribute to world music."

Whether folk music or art music, the decisive factor for the selection is above all the artistic value—the level of taste. "In art bad taste is a real spiritual illness. It is the duty of the school to offer protection against this plague. The school of today does not only neglect to do this, it actually opens doors and gates to the trash of music. In school, singing and music making must be taught in such a way that in the child for all his life a desire for noble music is awakened."

Right in the beginning of school music education stands the unaccompanied single voice song. Very early, in the third class, perhaps even before capability in reading notes in the second class, Kodály recommends the introduction of two-part singing. "Its resulting worth is invaluable, not only in respect to polyphonic hearing, but also to the perfection of one-voice singing. Singing in tune is only learnable by two-part singing. The two voices correct and balance each other.

"The simple instrumental accompaniment to unison melody develops a passable, unclear, and still insecure instinct for harmony. Polyphonic music, however, can only be perceived by our ears when we hear a different melody simultaneously, only when we have learned to sing an independent melodic line without the support of any accompaniment. In this way we come to an understanding of a musical style in which the voices do not sing only for themselves, but in which they assist and complement each other and thereby build a higher unit."

The rhythmic studies also must begin earlier and much more intensively than was formerly the case. Rhythm should likewise be studied in groups, that is, "two-voiced." The musical group study presents an advantageous educational media which the older schools unfortunately never used.

From the pentatonic two-voiced material by ways of easy diatonic polyphony instruction proceeds organically to the bicinia[1] of the old masters. "From there it is but one step to the two- and more-part polyphonic music of the great masters, and the wonderful realm of vocal music reveals itself to the astonished child. To the ear developed in this manner even instrumental music will no longer be a foreign language, despite the fact that one has not learned to play an instrument."

Obviously the gifted children should start to learn the instruments which they have some talents for. Singing however is possible for all and must therefore remain the basis of musical education. In addition to the classroom chorus and the school chorus, small vocal ensembles of three and four pupils should be established. These should try to sing at sight melodies of all styles without the assistance of instruments. This can be followed by two- and three-part songs. "Nothing can stimulate the general musical perception so much as the responsibility for singing an independent part by oneself."

Music education in school is in the same way responsible for the education of the whole society as well as for the elite. Both must be given equal consideration. "The greatest mistake of our culture is that it is built from the top down, and even this we do too quickly. Culture is the result of slow development. Hurrying it unduly, or changing the order of its development is impossible. Unfortunately, we have built the highly decorated towers first. Only when we discovered that the whole building was in danger to fall down we began to bolster up the foundation walls. Even yet the foundation is not correctly built."

The training of professional musicians has its problems also, but the problem of the music education of the public has not yet even reached the level of research and experiment. It must begin in the primary school. "The goal is: To educate children in such a way that they find music indispensable to life...of course good artistic music."

In professional music education Kodály strives for a connection between musical tradition and world outlook. "We must recognize all the worthwhile tradition of Western European music, but we must not educate mere Europeans but musicians who are at the same time Hungarian musicians. Only the blending of European and Hungarian tradition can achieve a result that is worthwhile and valid for the Hungarian nation. We must imbibe the Hungarian musical life through folk music if we are to compensate for the fact that it concerns itself with only a small community."

At the commemoration of the fifth anniversary of his friend Bartók's death, Kodály put this question "How shall we evaluate his legacy? The prerequisite for a final return of Bartók is a musically educated Hungary. All the factors must work together in order to achieve this if his art should finally reach those from whom it proceeded, the working folk, and is to be understood by them. Only then will there be a Hungarian musical culture."

Kodály's Musical Pedagogic Publications

(1) *Songs for little children—Fifty Nursery Songs.* Kodály has set fifty pentatonic melodies to words by Hungarian contemporary poets who came close to his endeavors. "The Songs for Little Children are set not in a cosmopolitan speech but in Hungarian musical language." The songs are

progressively arranged and do not go beyond the range of a sixth. The melodies proceed from two tones (Nos. 1–6) through three tones (Nos. 7–15) and four tones (Nos. 16–34) to the full pentatonic (Nos. 35–50).

The tone *do* should in no way be considered the central tone of these melodies. This may be observed in the different tonal order of the three-tone melodies (the underlined tone is always the tonic or principal tone):

No. 7 *m-r-d̲*; No. 8 *m-r̲-d*; No. 9 *r-d-l̲*; Nos. 10–12 *d-l̲,-s ,*; No. 13 *d-l-s̲ ,*; No. 14 *d̲-l,-s ,*.

Songs with modal tendencies are much in the majority. Those melodies which have do as a central tonic and tend to be in major, are in the minority.

In this way the fluctuating character of the pentatonic is emphasized much more than, for example, in the melodies of the Orff Music for Children.

(2) Pentatonic Music. This collection comprises four books with a content of 440 pieces. The melodies are notated only by syllables. Kodály hopes by this means to intensify the inner hearing, and to sharpen the tonal perception. The pentatonic melodies serve the teaching of perfect intonation, the development of musical perception, and the introduction to the understanding of Hungarian music.

Volume 1: 100 Hungarian Folksongs. The range of tones is slowly broadened from the third (*m-d*) through the fifth (*s-d*), sixth (*l-d; m-s,*) to the octave (*l-l; s-s,*) to the ninth (*l-s,*).

This extension takes place in the course of twenty songs. The major octave range (*d'-d*) is first reached in Nos. 23 and 24 and immediately dropped again. At the same time a similar extension of rhythm can be observed. For the first time syncopation occurs in No. 32, and in No. 36 the typical divided rhythm.

The first 48 songs are in duple metre. Nos. 49 and 69 present complex metres for the first time, and Nos. 90, 92, 98 are in 5/8 metre.

The introduction of "rubato" (free flowing rhythm) occurs in No. 63, and "parlando" (free rhythm in accordance with speech rhythm) in No. 74.

The final quarter of the volume contains up to the last song a forceful and logical organic increase in difficulty of rhythmic complexities.

Volume 2: One Hundred Little Marches. Kodály wrote these pieces in order to compensate for the lack of short folk melodies with simple rhythms in pentatonic tonality. "We need melodies for children which are in the spirit of folksongs but which lack their difficulty, and with which we can musically prepare the basis for the real folksongs."

With these melodies the children already learn some typical melodic patterns so that later they can feel at home with folksong and Hungarian music.

The 8–16 measure pieces encompass the range of the sixth, the octave, and the ninth, up to the tenth. The open tonal cadences on the changing principal tone of the pentatonic scale are characteristic.

Volume 3: One Hundred Tscheremissian Songs. The selection and graded arrangement of the melodies bespeak the experienced and goal-conscious pedagogue, especially through the gradual increase in tonal and rhythmic difficulties.

Volume 4: One Hundred Forty Tschuwachian Songs. At the conclusion of Volume 4, Kodály writes: "Whoever has conquered the rhythmic difficulties of the music of the Tschuwachian, Tscheremissian, and other Eastern peoples will easily overcome the complicated rhythms of modern music. The world vista will expand more and more and the restriction to a single national musical culture will disappear. The Tschuwachian melodies contain larger rhythmic irregularities, extraordinary metres and metric changes."

(3) 333 Reading Exercises—Introduction to Hungarian Folkmusic. This Hungarian Singing Primer explores a total of twenty different tonal organizations (modi or melodic patterns) in strict pentatonic. Within each melodic grouping there is a carefully planned increase in rhythmic difficulty. Particular rhythmic tensions (as the divided rhythm), complicated metres, and metric changes appear only in the last part of the book. This whole book of instruction contains no exercise in triadic harmony, neither in major nor minor. Exercises built on *do* as the tonic of the pentatonic appear first in No. 325.

"We need many reading exercises in order to have notated examples at hand which are continuously new and which have never been seen before. He who can recognize the principal interval more or less well does not yet read, he only spells.... One must read in whole concepts, first a word (motive), then more, grasp a whole phrase at once, and arrive at the details from a consideration of the whole. We should perceive the melody in its entirety before we sing it aloud."

The one-voice reading exercises can be used at every educational level as elementary materials.

Kodály recommends the following methodical procedure:

1. only clap the rhythm
2. sing the rhythm on a single tone

3. sing the melody on a syllable suitable for vocalization
4. sing the melody on sol-fa syllables

Later when the usual note names are introduced the transposition by tonic sol-fa syllables into different tonalities is possible. Rhythm should always have precedence since the main cause for bad note reading is to be found in rhythmic uncertainty.

In these melodies many descending skips are found. "Intervals are usually practiced in ascending skips even though it is much more difficult to sing them in the descending direction."

The *333 Reading Exercises* build a bridge from simple pentatonic children's songs to the rhythmically and tonally rich Hungarian folksongs with their distinctive characteristics of historical generation. "It is a wrong method to begin with diatonic melodies and only to take up the pentatonic later as if to return to a strange curiosity."

(4) Let Us Sing Correctly—Two-Part Song Exercises. This collection contains 107 short exercises as an introduction to two-part singing. The progressively ordered melodies avoid rhythmic difficulties and, with the exception of the last two, half-tone steps, so that concentration on perfection of intonation is not neglected. In the first exercises (Nos. 1–29) only one voice moves while the other remains as a bourdon (pedal) tone.

All exercises are repeated with an exchange of melodic line between the voices. If the tonal range permits it, the same key is used, otherwise a new tonality either higher or lower.

The exercises are hummed, or sung on vocalizing syllables, or with sol-fa syllables. Every instrumental accompaniment, above all the piano, is avoided.

If at the beginning the simultaneous attack of two voices is found to be difficult, the second voice can begin one half measure later. The less lively voice should always begin, however. "The training in perfect intonation is no superfluous pedantry. Such exercises are excellent for ear training and for richness and beauty in choral sound. Only a chorus with perfect intonation has real color and real polish. The good sound of combination tones is the proof, but at the same time the reward of correct singing." In the foreword Kodály explains in detail the further way to diatonic two-part singing (first the introduction of *fa* and then of *ti*).

(5) Bicinia Hungarica—Introduction to Two-Part Singing.

Volume I, Nos. 1–58: Seventeen folksong settings and forty-one original songs. Nos. 1–30 are pentatonic melodies and Nos. 31–58 are nonpentatonic with two exceptions. The melodic line is frequently exchanged between upper and lower voices. Some melodies are based on an ostinato. The rhythmic difficulties also are gradually increased in the two-part setting (syncopations, change of metres, compound metres and unusual metres: $\frac{5}{4}$, $\frac{7}{8}$).

Volume II, Nos. 59–97. 26 folksongs and 12 original melodies. Nos. 59–71 are pentatonic, No. 69 is bitonal, and No. 63 has changing metres.

Volume III, Nos. 101–20. There are no pentatonic songs. The collection contains Hungarian folksongs, some Geneva psalms, and other spiritual songs.

Volume IV, Nos. 121–80. All the melodies are pentatonic with three Finnish and seventeen Tscheremissian folksongs.

There is no difference of style between the Hungarian folksongs and the original songs by Kodály. He develops his individual polyphonic style, a kind of pentatonic counterpoint, completely and organically combined with the Hungarian melodies.

The 180 Bicinia should arouse the understanding for polyphony in order to lead to the beauty of polyphonic music and to the great choral works of world music literature.

The foreword indicates that Kodály wrote these much requiring Bicinia for children, for the school. "Folkschool in Galanta, my dear little barefooted playmates! I thought of you as I wrote these works. Your voices sounded to me through the fog of fifty years. If we years ago had learned such songs as these how different we might have formed our life in this small country. The recognition remains for those who now are starting to learn: There is not much worth in singing only for ourselves. It is much lovelier to sing together in two parts. Then the combined singing of hundreds and thousands will be unified in a great harmony."

(6) Little Bicinia. This is a selection from the Bicinia Hungarica.

Volume I, Nos. 1–35, contains twenty-nine songs out of Volume I, four out of Volume II, one out of Volume III of the *Bicinia Hungarica*, and one out of another collection. Volume I contains twenty-three pentatonic melodies.

Volume II, Nos. 1–29, contains seven songs from Volume I, eleven from Volume II, seven from Volume IV of the *Bicinia Hungarica*, and one from the *15 Two-Part Vocal Exercises*. Volume II contains nineteen pentatonic melodies.

(7) 15 Two-Part Vocal Exercises. This volume contains little inventions and a few fugal expositions. Simple pentatonic pieces (Nos. 1-5) make an easy path to expressive polyphonic two-part singing. The work is conceived, on the one hand, as a continuation of the Bicinia Hungarica and, on the other hand, as an introduction to Bertalotti's *50 Solfeggio-Exercises.* The pieces of Bertalotti can be considered as having the same significance for vocal as Bach's inventions have for instrumental schooling; the gaining of ability for judging and a certainty in stylistic questions. After intensive work with the two-part singing exercises and with Bertalotti, the pupil is capable of singing the greatest choral works of world musical literature. "This knowledge and capability also leads him to the understanding of instrumental music. The singing of a Vivaldi theme, or the simple singing of the principal themes brings the individual closer to the entire work than the best formal analysis."

(8) 22 Two-Part Vocal Exercises

(9) 33 Two-Part Vocal Exercises.

(10) 44 Two-Part Vocal Exercises.

(11) 55 Two-Part Vocal Exercises.

(12) 66 Two-Part Vocal Exercises.

The last five works continue on the way of overcoming the difficulties of polyphonic singing through the gradual and logical increase of difficulties. Introduction to chromaticism, complicated tonalities and meters, old clefs, and themes with wide range which approach instrumental proportions. The human voice is developed into an instrument which provides an approach to art music of all times by means of artistic polyphonic singing, and simultaneously developed ear training and musical perception. The door is open to the great works of music literature even for those who do not play an instrument. "These works only fulfill their purpose when they find an echo in the souls of millions."

Vocal education through an intensive solfège study is necessary also for the instrumentalist. "We must strive for a music making that rests on the basis of singing and springs from the spirit, rather than being based on the mechanical domination of the instrument and music making only with the fingers. Thus only one can hope that the musician will `sing' with his instrument."

The singing exercises are designed for the education of the musical lay person as well as the professional musician; for the general school as well as for the special music school. "We need better lay and professional musicians. What defines a good musician can be summarized in the following points: a trained ear, a trained voice, a trained intellect, a trained heart, and trained hands. All these capabilities must be developed simultaneously and always remain in balance."

In his lectures concerning the basic goals of present day music education Kodály frequently cites from Schumann's "Musical House and Life Rules": "The education of the ear is most important. Concern yourself very early with the recognition of tonality and tone! concern yourself, even if you have little vocal abilities, to sing from sight without accompaniment; the sharpness of hearing will be continuously improved in this way. You must pursue this until you understand the printed page. Sing regularly in a chorus, in particular a middle voice. This will make you musical. Listen eagerly to old folksongs, they are a mine of beautiful melodies."

(13) Tricinia. The twenty-nine three-part singing exercises with texts contained in this collection serve as an introduction to old and new polyphony and lead directly to the difficult choral works of Kodály and Bartók. No. 29 sounds like an introduction to one of Kodály's finest choral works (The Mountain Nights).

(14) Epigrams (without text).

(15) Epigrams (The same as 14, with text).
Kodály indicates these nine songs with piano accompaniment simply as "one voice reading exercises." Behind this indication are hidden masterworks which above all make high technical and musical demands. The song part is entirely independent of the piano accompaniment which through its modern harmony brings sharp dissonances to the vocal part.

As in the advanced two-part singing exercises the song part is here a kind of compromise between instrumental and vocal melody.

In a wider sense the fifty children and youth choruses also belong to the pedagogical works of Kodály. Among these, folksong settings and original works are to be found. In the works of smaller range one to two melodies are set together or varied. In the larger works several melodies are bound together to a whole. The major-minor tonalities are almost entirely avoided. Pentatonic and modal melodies dominate. Simple forms are in the majority in these children choruses.

Through relationships of the fifth, through imitation, and canonic-like voice leading a linear style is developed as an introduction to greater polyphony.

In the children's choruses by Kodály there are devices which are related not only to the choral settings but also to the simple piano pieces of Bartók. In Bartók's as well as in Kodály's pedagogical works one finds a "unity of pedagogic value and art value" displayed. In comparison to Bartók and Hindemith, and also to the great "pedagogic" composers of the past centuries the systematic and consistent musical didactic thinking and concern is convincing. For over 40 years Kodály continuously enriched the music education of our times with theoretic, organizational, and practical compositional works.

Kodály's educational reform plans and their actual realization in the music education of Hungary give again evidence of a systematic construction. The public school system and music school organization of Hungary are similarly structured of three levels: the elementary (Folk) schools correspond to elementary musical schools—the high schools (Gymnasium) correspond to conservatories of music—the university corresponds to the state academy of music.

In the eight years of general elementary school, music instruction for two hours per week is compulsory for all classes. A special type of elementary school, the musical elementary school, with a normal academic course of study and intensified music program consisting of a daily music class of one hour, guarantees the discovery and promotion of the musically gifted youth. Each of the six conservatories is connected to a special high school for music. Besides the normal elementary school and the musical elementary school, there are special elementary music schools devoted entirely to musical training, with a one year basic course and six years of further musical training. These schools prepare the gifted child for the conservatory. The conservatory educates in a five year program, choral singers and orchestral musicians (professional musicians), and prepares students for the state academy.

Every primary school teacher for the first four classes of the elementary school receives a many-sided musical training in a teachers' training school which also includes the learning of a required instrument.

In the upper grades of the elementary school, classes 5–8, a music specialist teaches. His study includes one principal instrument, music theory, music history, composition, teaching methods and practice. Those who have been trained in the conservatories for the elementary music school can also serve as special music teachers in all public elementary schools.

In the study program for music teachers in high schools who are trained at the state academy, there is a special emphasis on vocal training and choral directing, besides the normal courses of study. The study of folk music is an obligatory subject for all students of the conservatory and academy.

The Hungarian teacher-training system (also in the area of music) allows for an easy transfer from one level of instruction to another. Teachers trained for one type of school, e.g. elementary school, may take supplementary studies and become teachers in the high school. Such transfer facilitates professional careers.

But all these organizational efforts alone would not have been sufficient to achieve a general reform of music education in Hungary. Just as important were the didactic discussions in manifold reports and the publications of musical teaching material which, after 1937, led to an inner reform.

Within thirty years, Kodály published sixteen teaching works which in the whole present a complete music method based on singing and ear training. These publications—among them six collections of several volumes each with over one hundred exercises—include all levels of musical education from the kindergarten to the music academy, from the classroom choir of the primary school to the music academy choir, from the post-school singing group to the efficient amateur choir. Together with some fifty pieces for children and youth choirs the sixteen pedagogical works of Kodály comprise a comprehensive music pedagogic teaching work which makes possible an organic introduction to the choral compositions of Kodály and Bartók and to the large choral works of world musical literature. What Bartók achieved in the instrumental area—a music-pedagogic microcosm—Kodály achieved in the vocal music area. His exemplary vocal works are not only microcosmic patterns of his own style and therefore bridges to his complete oeuvre, but at the same time provide patterns for improvisation and invention which may build a bridge to modern music.

Notes

1. Bicinia: two-voiced songs by composers of the Renaissance period.

Folk Song in a Kodály-Based Curriculum

by Sister Lorna Zemke

A fundamental premise of Kodály's philosophy is that music and singing should produce pleasurable experiences, rather than boredom, for children. Kodály stressed the importance of fostering in children a desire for the kind of music that, because of its quality, would bring them a lifetime of meaningful experiences. He insisted on the teaching of music for appreciation and he believed this direction was not to be left to chance experiences; according to Kodály, the responsibility for this teaching belongs to the school, whose duty it is to organize such experiences.[1]

It must be emphasized that the basis of the entire Kodály approach is singing, which necessarily includes active musical participation. According to Kodály, singing is the foundation of all music and the voice the most accessible instrument to everyone. Through use of the voice in singing, it is possible to achieve both genuine musicianship and intellectual development.

As a natural result of Kodály's interest in singing and his in-depth research into Hungarian folk songs, he encouraged the use of folk song material for developing music appreciation and fostering musical literacy. The point of departure, then, is folk music: first the music of one's own nation and then that of other countries, following a progression that leads eventually to classical and composed music. Kodály's insistence on using folk songs, beginning with the education of very young children, is based on the belief that musical material must be both intelligible and artistic; folk songs possess these qualifications.[2]

Kodály reasoned that because folk music is the music of the people it contains the nuances of a nation's language in natural rhythmic and motivic selection, turns and lengths of melodic phrases, and perfection of form. On the basis of this premise, every country can use folk songs—not only as the foundation of music education but also as a means for transmitting a national culture to its people. "To write a folksong is as much beyond the bounds of possibility as to write a proverb. Just as proverbs condense centuries of popular wisdom and observation, so, in traditional songs, the emotions of centuries are immortalized in a form polished to perfection. The more of them we implant into young souls the more closely we link them to the nation."[3]

The American tradition of folk music is inexhaustible because of the richness and variety of cultures found within our borders. High-quality American folk songs and traditional children's singing games, dances, and nursery songs abound, and they provide a vast repertoire of suitable teaching material for use in the schools. Because of the extent of the American folk repertoire, the challenge of choosing suitable folk song material for teaching is a necessary but rewarding task. The major criteria for selecting songs for teaching consist, first of all, of researching the most authentic, typical folk songs of a culture and then choosing those that have the greatest artistic merit. Laszlo Vikar, eminent Hungarian ethnomusicologist, states that "variation" in folk song means "life," so the richness of the folk song is in the number of variants that song gathers.[4] Researchers generally agree that the authenticity of a folk song is confirmed by its variants.

According to Kodály, only the best music is suitable for children. What then are some guidelines for determining the quality of folk songs and their usability in a Kodály-based curriculum? One must examine the texts of each song to determine whether: (1) the topics/subjects are relevant for children; (2) the language is clear, direct and appropriate for children; and (3) the song would encourage imagination and creativity in children. One must then perform the song and determine whether: (1) text and tune fit well together for children and (2) the song is emotionally appealing and sets a mood to which children can respond.[5]

The folk song material itself determines the pedagogical sequence of a Kodály music education curriculum, and the skills of music reading and writing stem from an acquaintance with folk songs, just as the reading and writing of any national language is based upon its unique body of literature. The pluralistic society of America is made up of numerous and varied ethnic groups, all of which have valuable folk traditions. Selections from the folk repertoires of four major groupings (Anglo-American, African-American, Native American, and Hispanic-American) are used here to derive some musical learnings and to demonstrate some possible techniques for teaching these folk songs. The given folk songs are not intended to be taught sequentially but are isolated examples.

Anglo-American: *Risselty Rosselty*

I mar-ried my wife in the month of June, Ris-sel-ty Ros-sel-ty now, now, now! I car-ried her off by the light of the moon, Ris-sel-ty Ros-sel-ty now, now, now! Ris-sel-ty Ros-sel-ty Hey bom-bos-i-ty, Nick-i-ty, nack-i-ty, ret-i-cule qual-i-ty, Wil-low-by, wal-low-by now, now, now!

Musical Learnings:

Tone Set:
s, l, t, ⓓ r m f s

Scale:
Major (plagal)

Meter:
⁶⁄₈ with upbeat

Rhythm Patterns:

1.
2.

Melody Patterns:

1. s, d m r d l l, d s,
2. s, s, s, s, s, s, l d d d
3. m m m s f r l d d d r m

Form:
Verse/chorus with irregular phrasing, 4 + 3.

A   B
a a   b+a

Selected Techniques:
- Recite the rhythm of the song, using the syllables ♩ = ta; ♫♫ = ti ti ti; ♩. = ta-i. Do this while conducting a large two-beat pattern in ⁶⁄₈ (bring the arm down on beat one and up on beat two).

- Clap only on beat one and place the fingertips of both hands together on beat two while reciting the rhythm patterns.
- Prepare syllables of measures 3 and 4 by using hand signs.

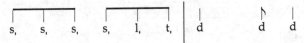

Sing, on pitch, the rhythm of all measures except those with this rhythmic pattern; have the students sing that pattern (with syllables, and while using hand signs) as it appears in the song.
- Discuss the verse/chorus form of the song; note the irregular number of phrases in the second section.
- Sing the entire song with syllables. On the board, add up all the sounds used in the song from the lowest to the highest (s, l, t, d r m f s), circle the tonic (*do* is F), and name the type of scale (major).
- Sing the song with words; have half of the class sing the verses and the other half sing the chorus.

Somebody's Knockin' at Your Door (Spiritual)

Musical Learnings:

Tone Set:
  1, (d) r m s l d'

Scale:
  do pentatone (extended)

Meter:
  $\frac{6}{8}$

Rhythm Patterns:

Melody Patterns:
  1. d d m I r d l̦ d I d I d
  2. s s d' I l s m s I s I s
  3. d' d' l I s l I m m r I d l̦

Form:

Selected Techniques:
- Discuss and demonstrate the recurring eighth-quarter-eighth syncopation pattern by tapping the beat with a foot and using

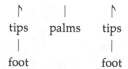

  fingertips and palms to perform the pattern.
- Tap the beat and recite "syn-co-pa" to the eighth-quarter-eighth pattern each time the pattern appears in the song; recite all other rhythms, using the syllables *ta-a* for a half note, *ta* for a quarter note, and *ti-ti* for two eighth notes.
- Observe the basic pattern of the song (eighth-quarter-eighth, eighth-eighth quarter) and have the class identify how many times and in which measures this pattern occurs. Point out the variant of this pattern (eighth-quarter-eighth, quarter, quarter); discuss the uniformity of rhythmic structure throughout the composition.
- Sing the syllables of the first two phrases (eight measures) of the song. Divide the class in half and have one group sing the syllables of the first phrase while the other group claps the melody's rhythm, forming a round to the singing, entering two measures after the entrance of the first group.

97

- Sing the second phrase of the song with words while students continue to clap the round.
- Note the similarities and differences between the phrases and identify the measures in which the clapping in a round seemed easier to perform (discuss the two tied half notes).
- Discuss the scale (*do* pentatonic , extended); divided the class and sing the song with words as a round.

Blue Corn-Grinding Song (Zuni Indian)

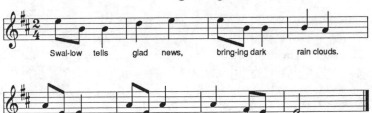

Swal-low tells glad news, bring-ing dark rain clouds.

Hi- ya- ho, hi- ya- ho, hi- ya- he.

Musical Learnings:

Tone Set:
   r m s l d' r'

Scale:
   re pentatone, extended

Meter:
   $\frac{2}{4}$

Rhythm Patterns:

   1.
   2.
   3.

Melody Patterns:
   1. r'l l l l d' r'
   2. s r r l s r s
   3. s m r l r
   4. A characteristic descending melodic line.

Form:

   A   Av
   ∧   ∧
   a aᵥ   aᵥbᵥ

98

Selected Techniques:

- Have the class walk to the beat, using a soft, shuffling step.
- Tap the beat on a drum while students recite the rhythm patterns (using *ta, ti-ti*).
- Clap/tap/patsch an ostinato (using the rhythm of a quarter note followed by two eighth notes) while students recite the song's rhythm.
- Sing the first phrase on the neutral syllable *loo* while the class accompanies with a two-finger clap on the rhythm patterns.
- Sing the syllables of the song; then repeat the song, singing the syllables on all eighth-note rhythms (but clap only on the quarter-note rhythms).
- Sing and discuss the interval of a perfect fourth in the first line (r'–l) and in the second line (s–r) and point out the importance of this interval in the song.
- Discuss the *re* pentatonic scale, drawing attention to the pairs of major seconds, separated by minor thirds, that form the scale.

Naranja Dulce (Sweet Orange; Mexican)

Na- ran- ja   dul-   ce, li- món par- ti-   do, da- me un a-

bra- zo que yo te   pi-   do.

1. O my sweet orange, my sweet orange, cut lemon,
   give me a hug which I asked of you, dear.

2. If you should think that I have deceived you,
   in just a while you'll forget about that.

3. Just play the March, for my heart is crying;
   Goodbye, señora, I'm going now, dear.

To play this singing game, the children form a circle with one child standing in the center. All of them, except the child in the middle, sing the first two stanzas. The child in the center sings the third stanza. Then, with the singing of the word "goodbye," he or she approaches someone in the circle and stretches out a hand in farewell. The selected person then becomes the one in the center of the circle as the game starts over.

Musical Learnings:

Tone Set:
s, (d) r m f s l

Scale:
do hexachord (extended)

Meter:
$\frac{3}{4}$

Rhythm Pattern:

♫♫ | ♩ ♩ | ♫ ♫

Melody Patterns:
1. s, d m l s s l s m l d d
2. m r d l r r f m r l d d

Form:
A–A$_v$

Selected Techniques:
- Write the rhythmic notation of this song on a long strip of paper or cardboard. Cut the measures (and incomplete measures) apart and mix them up; then, count the meter and clap the rhythm patterns as they occur in the song. Have the students put the cards in correct order.
- Draw a sol-fa or letter ladder on the board and ask students to sing the syllables and use hand signs as you point to the syllables or letters.

  l
  s
  f
  m
  r
  d
  s,

- Select seven students to represent the seven scale tones (six tones and one repetition—*ti* is not used in the song). Have students stand side-by-side in front of the room, and give each child a card with one note name on it. Walk behind the "people scale" and point out the melody of the song by pretending to tap the heads of the scale members while the class sings designated syllables.

- Have the class sing the entire song in syllables, reading from staff notation, while you play the I and V chords on the Autoharp, making appropriate chord changes.
- Have the students sing the roots of the chords (d and s for I and V) while you sing the words of the song.
- Compare the melodic patterns "s s l s m d d" and "r r f m r d." Add up all of the scale syllables and discuss the *do* hexachord scale (extended).
- Divide the class, and have half of the children sing the song while the rest play the game.

Kodály's insistence that music education include folk songs as its basic material is as valid today as ever. In Kodály's words, folk songs have the richest "variety of moods and perspectives" of any repertoire.[6]

The music culture of a country is not created by individual musicians, but by the whole population. Everybody has a share, even to the smallest. It is vain for individuals to work if they are not accompanied by the echo of millions. The compositions of every country, if original, are based on the songs of its own people. That is why their folksongs must be constantly sung, observed and studied. It is necessary to listen to other people's great classics as well. We can learn from them how they made use of folk music in their works. We can see that the better they succeeded in this, the better they were understood by humanity.[7]

Notes

1. Institute for Cultural Relations, *Musical Education in Hungary* (Budapest: Institute for Cultural Relations 1966), 3.

2. Tibor Sarai, "The Role of Music in the Life of Children and Youth." (Paper presented at the International Society for Music Education Conference, Moscow, USSR, July, 1970.)

3. Zoltán Kodály, *The Selected Writings of Zoltán Kodály*, n.p., 1974), 145.

4. Vikar, Laszlo, "Folk Song History and Research." (Presented in a class, Silver Lake College, Manitowoc, WI, Summer 1987.)

5. Eleanor Locke, suggestions presented during a session, "We're Bound Away: Capturing the Essence of a Bygone Era in Song," at the Twelfth Annual Conference of the Organization of American Kodály Educators, St. Louis, MO, March 1986.

6. Zoltán Kodály, "Folk Song in Pedagogy," *Music Educators Journal* 53, No. 7 (March 1967), 59–61.

7. _____, *Visszatekintes*, ed. Ferenc Bonis, 2 vols. (Budapest: Zenemukiado Vallalet, 1964), 222.

Can Kodály Help My Teaching?

by Alexander Farkas

At the core, Americans are a very practical people. We like to know how things work and what we can find to make our lives easier. We like to see results that can be measured. We like to know how long a job will take and what the final product will look like. We like to find shortcuts and solve our problems quickly.

Kodály stands, in contrast, as a visionary. His musical roots lie in the villages where he found the treasures of folk melody to which he paid homage all his life. All his creative energies were devoted to deepening and expanding the popular appreciation of his discovery. For Kodály, the musical value of the finely honed folk melody was qualitatively equal to the highly evolved works of Palestrina, Bach, or Haydn. In his view, a deep love of folk song makes us more susceptible to the great creations of our musical heritage. Music education, according to Kodály, is not at all a finite curriculum. It is a process that makes us recognize a lifelong need for musical satisfaction.

The Role of Music

Music makes us feel good, says Kodály; singing generates an especially good feeling; and singing in tune makes us feel even better. Singing together with others adds the feeling of community, and a group of people singing in tune in two, three, or four parts is truly exciting. Being able to read music makes this possible, and according to Kodály, the easiest way to bring about access to all this good feeling and excitement is to start early.

In short, Kodály's teachings contain the request to live with music as a part of our lives. The most natural way to do this, he would remind us, is by singing. To help us on our way he offers us a time-tested model: the songs and singing games of village children. This is the music that belongs to the children; it is their own. It rarely goes beyond the range of the

103

children's own voices, and is never too difficult for them, so they participate with great energy. Children find a great deal of musical gratification in these songs.

Childhood is by nature its own place, whether in today's city or yesterday's town. It has its own needs, which have over the years increasingly moved with the child into our schools. Needs once satisfied spontaneously outdoors are now answered by a trained adult in the classroom. The music teacher is the living link with the child's own musical heritage. By showing love for the beauty of simple melodies, the music teacher provides the materials that become the child's own source of musical satisfaction. The melodies themselves, graceful and clean, encourage clear singing and good intonation. Upon this foundation, says Kodály, we can slowly build a place for music.

Folk Melodies

Kodály's observed that the folk melodies of young children often resembled the music of a much earlier time, a time before the diatonic system came into everyday use. These melodies contain no half steps. They are built simply on three, four, or five tones and contain no reference to triadic harmony. These pentatonic melodies, according to Kodály, are the ones children are best able to sing in tune.

The consistent use of pentatonic song materials strengthens musical skills. Since pentatonic music is based structurally on perfect intervals, we are continually practicing good intonation as we sing. It lends itself easily to the addition of a second voice, either as a pedal-drone or in imitation. We can thereby make the transition to two-part singing, which further encourages good intonation. From its simple lines, we can most easily introduce the study of form and derive the elements of notation, both rhythmic and melodic. The transition to diatonic materials passes so smoothly as to be hardly noticed, after which the two systems live comfortably side by side.

Solmization

On an early visit to England, Kodály was introduced to the use of tonic sol-fa, or relative solmization. This practice was devised by John Curwen to enable singers with little or no formal musical training to read their respective parts more easily at the weekly rehearsal of their local choral society. In the same way that many scientific discoveries have led to further advances unforeseen at the time, Kodály was able to understand the more important advantages made available through the use of Curwen's simple learning device: since any two syllables always define the same interval, relative solmization strengthens our intonation. Of even greater importance is the fact that the syllable of any given tone defines its position and function in the scale. As this syllable/function relation remains constant in any key, relative solmization becomes a most useful means of teaching harmony. The teachers of many of our theory classes have yet to realize the advantages of applying this simple tool.

Kodály most admired music in which each voice is of equal importance. The choral works of Palestrina, where every line shows exquisite melodic contour, supplied the models that he himself emulated. Page by page, through the course of Kodály's many two-part singing exercises, we are led gently from simple play-songs to sophisticated compositions worthy of performance. Each line is crafted with utmost care and blends with its partner in a way that encourages us, while singing our own part, to hear the other voice. As Bartók did with his *Mikrokosmos* for piano, Kodály gives us a pedagogy, not in words, but in music.

We may say that the best teaching goes unnoticed. The students are guided ever so gently to new areas of skill and awareness. Transitions are brought about smoothly. The course of a good lesson feels like a pleasant walk in good weather. The teacher is a musician-guide. If we choose to follow Kodály's varied path of musical pedagogy, we will find that he tells us not so much what to do, but rather what to become. The contours of his melodies shape our musical aesthetic. His polyphony improves our intonation. We will find greater faith in our own skills, for surely Kodály himself placed the greatest faith in teaching musicians.

Sound and Satisfaction

In the end it is the quality of sound that says everything. We may from time to time become overly concerned with the devices of teaching. Hand-signs and rhythm syllables, while most useful, do not in themselves make music. Results from tests of aural discrimination and rhythmic alertness do not reflect a child's need for musical satisfaction. While reading skills, most important, make available to us the vast body of musical literature, the music itself exists only in sound that is brought into being by the teacher. It is the teacher's own hearing that determines the intonation, shape, and overall quality of the children's singing.

Clearly implicit in Kodály's pedagogic vision is the premise that the teacher's own musical skills be strengthened first. The truest, most secure intonation must reside in the teacher's ear. We are asked to work without relying on the piano or other instruments. A steadiness of rhythmic pulsation must reside securely in the body. The teacher must be a capable, clear conductor, able to hear each vocal line equally. He or she must instill a level of comfort in breathing and be a model of vocal clarity. When these skills are secure, we become aware of what we wish to teach. With our musical priorities in functioning order, we know better how to proceed. In short, Kodály said that we strengthen our teaching by strengthening our teachers first.

The elements are simple, as are the aims: elegance of line, of harmony, and of parts. In balancing the elements, we achieve a sense of musical well-being so satisfying that we wish to experience it repeatedly. Only then do we come to realize that music is a necessary part of our lives. This, according to Kodály, is music education in its most significant form.

A pleasurable experience is one to which we return happily. Any melody that brings gratification endears itself to us. Whatever we know well is, in fact, a part of our being and is readily available at any time. To learn is to gladly make something a part of ourselves, because we quite logically wish to possess what is appealing to us. If we can easily perform an activity, we do so readily. A technique is secure when we no longer think about it: to sing a melody in tune means that we cannot sing it in any other way.

Can Kodály help my teaching? The question is deceptively simple. We need not search in haste for a reply, but we do know where the answer is to be found: in the skillful and elegant singing of our children.

PART THREE
Carl Orff

Photograph courtesy MMB Music, Inc.

The Orff Approach

by Beth Landis and Polly Carder

The central idea on which Carl Orff based his approach to music education is that music, movement, and speech are inseparable, and that they form a unity Orff called elemental music. He had observed that when children express themselves in natural and unstructured situations, they use music, movement, and speech together rather than separately. A child who is dancing often sings or chants; when a child sings, he or she often moves in rhythm with the singing. Orff used the word elemental to mean primal and rudimentary, and to refer to personal expression made naturally through music.

During the period in which Orff was developing his musical and educational work, there was a rather widespread theory that the historical development of music is reenacted in the life of each individual. The child was considered a primitive being, whose early musical responses were like those that ethnomusicologists see in the peoples of less sophisticated cultures.

Orff determined that music education should begin with the simplest concepts and the simplest songs, those most suitable to the child. A gradual, cumulative sequence of learning experiences resulted from this assumption. Ideally, the study should begin in early childhood and should make use of the child's own musical experiences as material for the instructional process. The child's own name, familiar words, sayings, and quotations are used in rhythmic chanting and in singing. The child hears his or her name spoken rhythmically, then sings it, and later reads and writes its rhythm in notation. Melodic intervals are learned as are rhythm patterns through singing them, saying them, moving to them, and playing them. Instruments are used from the earliest sessions in the course. By taking a simple motive, repeating it, and building on it, the child is able to succeed from the beginning. The child is using simple materials, and is able to develop them into something satisfying.

Orff found in the Eurhythmics of Jaques-Dalcroze more than one principle he was able to share. Most important of these in its effect on Orff's work was the idea that rhythm is the strongest of the elements of music; that the most innate and most natural musical responses of the human personality are rhythmic in nature; and that the logical starting point for education in music is rhythm. Through his concept of elemental music, Orff planned to make this idea work. Since rhythm is the shared element in speech, movement, and music, it is the logical starting point in the *Schulwerk*. (The first published collection of his instructional materials was titled *Orff-Schulwerk: Music for Children*. The Orff approach itself is often called "the *Schulwerk*."

The belief that rhythm is the vital element in music led directly to the development of a special ensemble of instruments. In the Orff philosophy, as in that of Jaques-Dalcroze, the study of piano, violin, and other standard instruments should be preceded by the development of certain musical skills: singing with accuracy and ease, moving precisely and moving creatively to music, and simple improvisation, among others.

In the Orff method, creativity is vitally important. His instructional plan includes provisions for several kinds of original work on a continuing basis. Children explore the sounds of words, melodies, and instruments. They choose or invent rhythmic and melodic fragments and use them to create accompaniment figures, introductions and codas, perhaps a whole song. The early instructional activities are like musical games, and indeed, they are often built on children's traditional games. The teacher should be prepared to help children notate their musical ideas, evaluate the music they produce, and relate their creative efforts to the study of musical form and style. Orff's description of his educational plan included the suggestion that teachers who are themselves creative, flexible, and open to new ideas are best suited to fostering these characteristics, inherent in the approach itself, in their students.

> Every phase of *Schulwerk* will always provide stimulation for new independent growth; therefore it is never conclusive and settled, but always developing, always growing, always flowing. Herein, of course, presents a great danger, that of development in the wrong direction. Further independent growth presupposes basic specialist training and absolute familiarity with the style, the possibilities and the aims of *Schulwerk*.[1]

Elemental music is intensely personal, based on communicative performance. Its materials are ideally the musical ideas of the children themselves, with the *Schulwerk* compositions as models and a carefully planned melodic and rhythmic vocabulary as a framework. It is primal, childlike, natural, and physical, drawing on the activities of the child at play for beginnings and points of reference in the teaching process. The concept of elemental music includes the assumption that a child relives, through his or her learning experiences, the musical development of mankind. The child's earliest musical experiences, then, are primordial: calls, cries, and chants, stamping, bending, and whirling. In elemental music, speaking, singing, and moving are not separate acts, but like the most natural, genuine musical expression, they become a composite.

The instructional materials Orff prepared for publication were intended to preserve his ideas and to transmit them to his students and other followers. They were written during the process of carrying out a series of broadcasts with Bavarian children, and after some years of teaching in which his philosophy had been formulated and his procedures shaped. As in the Dalcroze method, creativity in the form of improvisation was a major goal of the program. Also like Jaques-Dalcroze, Orff had definite ideas about how improvisation would be carried out. He stated often and emphatically that the songs he wrote for children's classes were intended only as models.

Several characteristics that were inherent in Orff's philosophy of music and education were clearly evident in his instructional materials: (1) The pentatonic mode was used throughout the entire first volume of the *Schulwerk*. (2) Ostinato patterns and *borduns*, which he expected children to create in their classroom, were consistently used as accompaniment in the model pieces provided. (3) Like Kodály, Orff conceived his approach to music education for children of his own geographical area and built upon musical material basic to their childhood experience. As the *Schulwerk* spread to other parts of the world, Orff made it clear that teachers in each culture should use the music of their own heritage and idiom. (4) Motives were often taken from songs and used in the introduction and accompaniment of those songs. (5) The distinctive Orff ensemble of instruments was used. (6) A basic part of the idea of elemental music is seen in the published volumes of *Schulwerk*—the chants and calls of childhood, especially the so-called universal chant of childhood (the descending minor third) are used in the beginning. It is apparent that Orff sought the early, simple experiences in the child's musical life as a beginning point for formal instruction. The arrangement of learning experiences in a gradual progression from simple to difficult is apparent in the written materials. (7) Speech patterns, beginning with single words and progressing to more complex activities such as speech canons, are presented in the published *Schulwerk*.

111

The day is now over

Orff. D. H. translation

chil - dren are pray - ing for care through the night. Then our

heav - en - ly Fath - er throws op - en the gate and

sends down His an-gels to watch o'er their fate.

"The Day is Now Over," from *Orff-Schulwerk Music for Children*, © B. Schott's Sohne, Mainz, 1956. © renewed. All Rights Reserved. Used by permission of European American Music Distributors Corporation, sole U.S. and Canadian agent for B. Schott's Soehne.

"The Day Is Now Over" from *Music for Children*, Volume I, illustrates important characteristics of the Orff instructional repertoire:

- Ostinato patterns are used extensively and help to develop independence and interdependence of voices (parts). The combination of several ostinatos is a frequently used device that involves several players in addition to the singers, and helps to develop ensemble playing.
- Like most of the songs Orff published for instructional use, this one appears in a complete and symmetrical setting with introduction and accompaniment. (Many of the songs also have codas.)
- The simplest of motives, extracted from the melody itself, are used to create the introduction and the accompaniment, the same way he intends that students create their own settings.
- The pentatonic mode can be used in a texture made of several lines (six in this case) without substantial dissonances.
- The delicate quality evident in both orchestration and text is found in many examples from the published *Schulwerk* repertoire.
- The "orchestration" is typical of *Schulwerk* pieces.

Speech

Speech as a part of the musical experience is a distinguishing characteristic of the Orff-*Schulwerk* approach. Orff made this a part of his plan because he felt that a gradual progression from speech patterns to rhythmic activities, and then to song is most natural for the child. The planned sequence begins with speech, continues with body rhythms such as clapping or tapping, and culminates in the playing of instruments. Orff facilitated the process by turning nursery rhymes, calls, chants, and traditional sayings into musical experiences. Each teacher is expected to make use of the nursery rhymes, sayings, and children's names that are already familiar to his or her class. Children create music based on the rhythm patterns of these and other words. For example, sometimes teachers list the first names of some of the children, and the class organizes these in an order that produces interesting rhythms, then set them to music. Alternately, short phrases may be built from the rhythm patterns of some of the names.

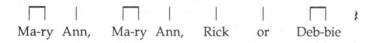

Concepts such as meter, accent, and anacrusis are introduced in speech patterns, reinforced in other activities, and then studied in a musical context. For example, the concept of canon is very effectively introduced through speech. Groups of children chant a phrase or sentence that is made up of interesting, varied rhythms. Using the idea of a round, one group begins and, at a point where rhythmic contrast has been noticed, the second group begins. The third group begins when the second has reached the predetermined point. Children caught up in the creative process will produce an endless variety of words, phrases, household sayings, and rhymes that can be used in the teaching process. When they are learning the names of places, colors, days of the week, flowers, and the like, they can use these words in repeated patterns or in interesting combinations. Complex or unusual rhythms should not be avoided if they are present in normal speech patterns and already somewhat familiar to the child. Children are flexible enough to adapt readily to changing meters and polyrhythms, and they can accept these complexities as naturally as they do the more traditional rhythmic patterns.

When the teacher presents word rhythms in notation, he or she must take care that these rhythms are represented with precision. Care also should be taken, however, not to distort the natural rhythms of speech by forcing them into preconceived duration patterns. For example, when the goal is to show the relationship between the durations of notes and the durations of names or other words, it is important not to change one to fit the other. One-syllable names like Anne and Jim, if used to illustrate whole-note durations, lose their natural, spoken duration.

In repeated chanting, clapping or tapping, singing, and playing of rhythms that were introduced through speech, the teacher must be sure that a given rhythm pattern is performed with consistent accuracy. This should not preclude experimentation to discover alternative rhythmic possibilities. While the children are studying rhythmic concepts through speech, other essential ideas may be introduced through the same medium. Phrasing, dynamic qualities, staccato, and legato may be discovered in this way. Emerging understandings of musical form—repetition, contrast, simple binary, ternary, and rondo forms—also can be developed through speech activities. Some concepts that would be quite difficult when encountered for the first time in a musical setting, where melody, dynamics, and other musical events occur simultaneously, can be introduced more successfully through word rhythms and then transferred to the abstract musical context. Rhythmic concepts are reinforced by combining speech patterns with body rhythms—also called sound gestures—clapping, stamping, finger snapping, and *patschen* or leg-slapping. In the following example, the eighth-note pattern to be clapped by Group I might be introduced through the rhythm of the word "forbidden" (see the accompanying example).

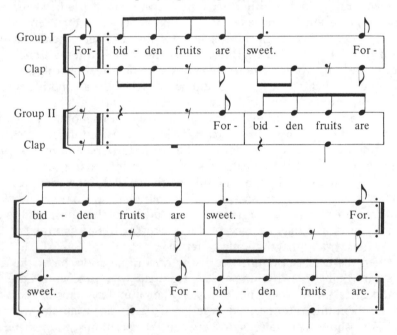

"Forbidden Fruits are Sweet," from *Orff-Schulwerk Music for Children,* © B. Schott's Soehne, Mainz, 1956. © renewed. All Rights Reserved. Used by permission of European American Music Distributors Corporation, sole U.S. and Canadian agent for B. Schott's Soehne.

Singing

Speech, chant, and song are all points along a single continuum. Singing experiences follow directly from speech: thus, melody grows out of rhythm. The child chants single words, phrases, and nursery rhymes. He or she claps these rhythm patterns and plays them on instruments. Children discover that their voices rise and fall in pitch as they chant. At this point the transition is made from speaking to singing. From that time on, speech and song reinforce and complement each other in the learning experience.

The earliest experiences in singing resemble play: children call back and forth, singing each other's names. Call-and-response games and songs based on counting-out rhymes develop. The teacher uses these activities to build concepts. He or she sings a musical phrase and the children learn by imitation. The teacher encourages a singing dialogue and notates the sounds children make in calling to each other. These sounds are played on the tuned instruments and become materials for creative work. Practice in speaking, chanting, and clapping word rhythms prepares the child for the experience of combining these rhythms, by now familiar, with melody. The earliest songs in *Music for Children* illustrate the meaning of Orff's term "elemental music." They are rudimentary, written in the singsong style that children use naturally. The following example from the supplementary material in volume 1 of the collection shows how word rhythms become a basis for musical rhythm, how natural pitch inflections develop into the simplest kind of melody, how the universal *so–mi* (5–3) chant of childhood becomes a rudimentary song, and how the words of a song relate to familiar occurrences in daily life.

Go to bed, Tom, Go to bed, Tom, Tired or not, Tom, Go to bed, Tom.

From the first page onward, songs in *Music for Children* are scored for accompaniment by instruments or by body rhythms or both. There are instrumental compositions without any vocal parts, but aside from simple chants like the one above, there are no songs without accompaniment or

117

independent instrumental parts. There is a strict, preplanned sequence for the introduction of melodic intervals. Singing begins with the descending minor third, *so–mi* (5-3). Other tones are added in the following order: *la, re, do* (6, 2, 1), to complete the pentatonic scale in volume 1, and then *fa* and *ti* (4, 7) in volume 2. Published repertoire beyond volume 1 includes examples in major and minor as well as Dorian, Phrygian, Lydian, and Mixolydian modes.

The pentatonic mode is used because Orff believed it to be most appropriate to the mental development of the young child. In this mode, children can improvise several melodic lines at the same time without dissonance and with less pulling toward the tonal center than in major and minor keys. In the Orff sequence of instruction, major and minor scales are postponed until later, when they are explored extensively. A corollary to the development of a child's natural expression is an appreciation for many kinds of tone relationships. Modes and non-Western scales can be as natural to the child as the diatonic system. Likewise, the student's own choice of chord progressions may go beyond those admitted in traditional Western music. Exposure to such sound relationships will contribute to the development of a greater melodic and harmonic sensitivity, which will find its full release in improvisation. The child will be prepared to accept and enjoy contemporary as well as traditional music.

"The Day Is Now Over" (see pp. 112-114) is typical of the Orff pentatonic song settings. It also illustrates several other characteristics of his instructional music. Ostinato patterns, used so extensively in these pieces, help to develop linear thinking and independence in performing one of the parts in an ensemble. The combination of several ostinatos is a frequently used device, involving several players in addition to the singers, and encouraging ensemble playing. Another feature of this example is that Orff has used the simplest of motives, extracted from the melody itself, to create the introduction and the accompaniment. He intended that students create their own settings in much the same way. Like most of his instructional songs, this one appears in a complete and symmetrical setting with introduction and accompaniment. (Many of the songs also have codas.) The instrumentation has a refinement and transparency found in many *Schulwerk* examples.

Bordun accompaniments are used extensively in Orff's exercises because their open fifths, like the droning of a bagpipe, act as a foundation for pentatonic melodies; these drone basses become good accompaniments to improvised melodies as well. The *bordun* tones also begin to suggest tonal center relationships. In some *Schulwerk* compositions, one or both tones of the *bordun* move up or down, and ostinato patterns develop out of *borduns* by means of embellishment or melodic figuration using neighboring tones.

Movement

Carl Orff wrote, "My idea and the task that I had set myself was a regeneration of music through movement, through dance."[2] Movement in the Orff approach begins with elemental movement; untrained, natural actions, common to all children. The enjoyment of this movement parallels the child's enjoyment of making music in his or her own way. Such movements as running, skipping, turning, hopping, and jumping—often thought of as play—are part of musical development in the Orff plan. The teacher encourages these movements, relates them to music, and uses them in building musical concepts. According to Dorothee Guenther, small children everywhere enjoy and explore movement for its own sake. There is much rhythmic activity without apparent purpose. Left alone, the child hops over imaginary obstacles, runs a few steps and stops abruptly, walks on tiptoe, and whirls until dizzy. These, she states, are valid ways of expressing feelings and of discovering the possibilities of creative movement. Unfortunately, they are usually stifled in early childhood.[3] In the teaching process, the freedom and joy of exploring movement should be preserved. Movement and improvisation foster greater self-awareness and help the child to actualize his or her expressive potential. Also, the development of perception not only will contribute to a firm foundation in music education but will provide the roots for a lifetime of continuing aesthetic education.

"Some music evokes a spontaneous response in movement, appealing primarily to an unconscious motivation—a motivation that is, in the actions of children, as yet untrained."[4] Children select patterns in movement and perform them as part of a composition they are singing and playing. Free, interpretive movement is performed by one child, a few, or an entire group. Many songs in the five volumes of *Music for Children* lend themselves to creative dramatization, and some are linked with instrumental pieces that could well accompany dancing. The four body rhythms (clapping, stamping, finger-snapping, and *patschen*) serve several purposes. They provide a way for children to sense rhythms through movement in addition to hearing them; they are used extensively to accompany singing and chanting; and they give practice in performing rhythms, developing a skill that is then transferred to the playing of the percussion instruments. Through body rhythms and in other movement, the basic concepts of musical form may be introduced. A pattern of clapping and stamping, for example, can become a theme. It can be repeated, varied, performed backward, performed antiphonally, or used as the basis for a rondo.

In the teacher-training program at the Orff Institute in Salzburg, courses in various aspects of movement comprise a major portion of the curriculum. Movement in Orff-*Schulwerk* is derived from Dalcroze Eurhythmics, but unlike Eurhythmics, it is not the central focus through which all or most musical study is approached. Children do use dance movements to interpret in their own ways the music they hear; they learn specific exercises in which they use ropes, balls, and other objects; specific rhythm patterns, tempos, and dynamic qualities are introduced through movement; and children have opportunities to improvise increasingly complex movements in response to music.

Improvisation

The primary purpose of music education, as Orff sees it, is the development of a child's creative faculty which manifests itself in the ability to improvise. This cannot be achieved by supplying ready-made (and usually much too sophisticated) material of the classical variety, but only by helping a child to make his own music—on his own level, integrated with a host of related activities. Speaking and singing, poetry and music, music and movement, playing and dancing are not yet separated in the world of children, they are essentially one and indivisible, all governed by the play-instinct which is a prime mover in the development of art and ritual. We find close parallels to this in archaic cultures and in the so-called primitive stages of our own civilization. It has been suggested that much of children's pleasure in nursery tales may arise "from an unconscious sympathy between the child and the thought and custom of the childhood of civilization." Nursery rhymes and tales have been discovered to be of incredible antiquity; not a few date back to prehistoric times. What are their musical equivalents? It is from this point of view that we shall recognize the value of repetitive patterns, which correspond to the endless repetitions in songs and tales and singing games; that we shall understand the insistence on pentatonic tunes (which represent the deepest layer of folksong) and on the primary importance of Rhythm: motor impulses manifested themselves earlier, and are still stronger, than melodic impulses.[5]

In Orff-*Schulwerk*, creativity most often takes the form of improvisation. Active participation as a member of a performing group is part of the Orff concept of elemental music. The student is expected to improvise freely: this is a consistent practice in Orff classes. All the activity areas within the *Schulwerk* are media for improvisation—movement, speech, body rhythms, singing, and especially the instruments (pitched and nonpitched). Students create rhythmic and melodic patterns, accompaniment figures, introductions, and codas for songs. The Orff instruments lend themselves to improvisation in the classroom. Orff's followers do not expect the masterful improvisation of a trained musician: the goal of extemporaneous performance is rather to form the habit of thinking creatively. The compositions Orff and Keetman developed for children's classes are intended to serve as models for children's (and teachers') own innovative work. To encourage creativity on the part of each child, the teacher provides conditions and opportunities for improvisation. Instead of suggesting musical materials and what to do with them, he allows the students to determine the form and content of the composition they are creating. Children find real satisfaction in manipulating musical materials.

Teachers in the Orff approach encourage self-evaluation, experimentation, and critical listening when children are improvising. Careful listening and a degree of aesthetic judgment are developed in this process. Each child must have opportunities to improvise, often using the special instruments, and to evaluate what he or she has produced. Beginning with simple experiences related to play, improvisation continues throughout the instructional sequence. As children build their improvisations in the style of the *Schulwerk*, they use the compositional devices, such as *bordun* and ostinato, that Orff suggested. A favorite simple form for improvisation is the rondo. This is because its structure becomes a useful framework: the theme is performed by all members of the group and alternated with contrasting improvised sections by individuals or small groups. The instruments children use were chosen or designed with improvisation, as a learning process, in mind. The timbres blend well and the instruments offer an interesting range of possibilities for playing the types of musical patterns on which improvisation, in this approach, is based. "Sleep, Baby, Sleep" (beginning on p. 122) shows some of the ways in which musical ideas are used in the model *Schulwerk* pieces, with the goal of helping children to create their own songs. The vocal line is first presented in unison, then in thirds with the melody on top, and finally in sixths with the melody as the lower line. The thirds for alto glockenspiel suggest a rocking motion well suited to the words.

Instruments

Special instruments are a distinctive feature of Carl Orff's instructional approach, distinguishing it from other methods. Emphasis on rhythm as the strongest of the constituent elements of music led to the development of the specially designed percussion instruments. With the cooperation of experts in the history and building of musical instruments, Orff developed an instrumental ensemble of mellow, delicate timbre (see the article "The *Schulwerk*—Its Aims and Origins" by Carl Orff, reprinted in this book).

Sleep, Baby, sleep

Soprano Glockenspiel

Alto Glockenspiel

Alto Glockenspiel

Alto Xylophone

Bass

pizz.

Sleep, ba - by, sleep! Thy

fa-ther guards the sheep. Thy mo-ther shakes the dream-land tree And

from it fall sweet dreams for thee. Sleep, ba-by, sleep! Thy

fa-ther guards the sheep.

Sleep, ba - by, sleep, the

124

large stars are the sheep,   The wee stars are the lambs I guess, The

fair moon is   the shep-her-dess: Sleep,   ba-by, sleep! The

large stars are the sheep.

Sleep, ba - by, sleep, Down

where the wood-bines creep, Be al-ways like the lamb so mild, A

kind and sweet and gen - tle child. Sleep, ba - by, sleep.

"Sleep, Baby, Sleep" from *Orff-Schulwerk Music for Children*, © B. Schott's Soehne, Mainz, 1956. © renewed. All Rights Reserved. Used by permission of European American Music Distributors Corporation, sole U.S. and Canadian agent for B. Schott's Soehne.

These are genuine musical instruments, not toys. The instruments are simple to play, are of excellent quality, and are more closely related to the instruments of non-Western cultures (such as those of the Indonesian *gamelan*) than to the percussion section of the modern symphony orchestra. The barred percussion instruments are soprano, alto and bass xylophone; soprano and alto glockenspiel; and soprano, alto, and bass metallophone. All are played with mallets. There is a wooden resonating chamber on each instrument, and tone bars can be removed to create specific scale patterns. The instruments most commonly used in the elementary classroom are diatonic, but extra bars are available for F♯ and B♭, thus making available three major and three minor keys. Chromatic instruments of the same type are also available. Other nonpitched instruments (drums, cymbals, triangles, and so forth) are considered resources for use with the ensemble.

Stringed instruments such as guitar or cello may be used along with the barred percussion instruments to play ostinatos and drones of a contrasting timbre. Simple patterns on the piano, used sparingly, may be an effective addition. Recorders are frequently used as melody instruments along with the ensemble, and at the more advanced levels of *Schulwerk*, independent recorder ensembles provide an expanded opportunity for students to develop musical skills. The special barred percussion instruments suit the physical development of children, since they require primarily large-muscle movements.

It is part of the *Schulwerk* plan that children be taught to play correctly. Instruments are often used as an extension of speech, singing, and movement activities. Often children can state musical ideas less self-consciously with instruments than they could with singing. Children can play rhythmic and melodic figures and learn to manipulate them in many ways. By playing instruments, children can participate in ensembles and begin to understand such musical principles as homophony and polyphony.

The instruments may, however, become too large a part of the instructional program. Teachers should use them sparingly, recognizing that "they are primarily an extension of the child's own singing, speaking, and moving. The desire to play the instruments is often very strong, demanding a sensitivity on the part of the teacher to make the right choice at the right time."[6]

Beginning with the simplest elements, and using performance as a mode of learning, Orff's plan leads to the playing of some challenging music. The accompanying "No. 46" canon shows that Orff has avoided drill and exercises as such, substituting a miniature composition. Its simple individual parts add up to an interesting whole. It is one of the culminating experiences in Volume I of *Music for Children*.

Canon A canon for glockenspiels. The instrumentation may be varied.

"Canon #46," from *Orff-Schulwerk Music for Children*, © B. Schott's Soehne, Mainz, 1956. ©
renewed All rights Reserved. Used by permission of European American Music Distributors
Corporation, sole U.S. and Canadian agent for B. Schott's Soehne.

Orff considered playing one of the specially designed instruments from memory to be far more suitable for the young child than the study of piano or any of the instruments that require simultaneous reading of musical notation, familiarity with the nature of the instrument, and the complex process of performance. Orff's plan that children learn from the beginning to play from memory frees them from the demands of concurrently playing, reading notation, and coordinating their performance with that of others. Notation is read from the early stages of the course, but it is introduced when it is needed as a means of storing and communicating musical ideas. This differs from the traditional study of music, in which memorization is a culminating activity. In the Orff approach, singing and playing are not dependent on musical scores, and memorizing is a natural beginning skill. Children use imitation, improvisation, and other creative techniques in addition to reading notation. The private study of piano and orchestral or band instruments is postponed until the child has acquired a backlog of musical concepts in addition to certain skills. As Orff put it:

> Children should always play from memory—only this will guarantee a maximum of freedom—but notation should not be disregarded; on the contrary, it should be introduced right at the beginning (together with speech-patterns for which rhythmical notation is sufficient) so that the child may jot down any rhythmic or melodic idea that occurs to him or her.[7]

Historical Development

Orff became involved with music education during the 1920s, when Emile Jaques-Dalcroze was making his startling innovations. He was influenced by Jaques-Dalcroze's thinking and by the same factors that had helped to shape it: the possibility of breaking away from the traditional methods and materials of the conservatory style of music education, a surge of interest in physical training and gymnastics, and the appearance of a new kind of dancing that has since become known as modern dance. The two men shared an interest in the theater, and Orff worked in the opera houses of Mannheim and Darmstadt. In this period a number of schools for training in gymnastics and dance were opened. Orff's Guentherschule, founded in 1924 in Munich in collaboration with Dorothee Guenther, was unlike most schools in that its purpose was to combine the study of music with the study of gymnastics and dance.

> As the *Schulwerk* instrumental and dance teaching developed, so also did the musical materials designed for it. All the dancers were expected to play all the instruments, and all instrumentalists were expected to dance. Guenther and Orff believed that, as a result of this interchange, sensitivity to the elements of music was heightened and response made more dynamic.[8]

Photograph courtesy of Studio 49, Graefelfing, Germany

This unification of movement and music was the key to Orff's concept of music education. His years of teaching experience confirmed the inseparable nature of music and dance, and culminated in an instructional approach based on his theory of elemental music. His students at the Guentherschule were not, as a rule, preparing for careers in music. Most of them were amateurs in music, preparing to become teachers of physical education, so Orff was challenged by the need to begin their training with the simplest rudiments.

Orff was in an excellent position to experiment with materials and methods of his own devising. *Schulwerk* began as an active, group approach to teaching the elements of music. Teaching in the Guentherschule, Orff sought the earliest and most basic learning experiences within the art. In 1930, the first edition of the *Schulwerk*, "Rhythmic and Melodic Exercises," was published. Like many other educators, Orff thought of books as a means of storing and preserving ideas created in the teaching process that might otherwise be overlooked or forgotten.

In World War II, the Guentherschule and the special instruments were destroyed, and Orff's work as an educator was temporarily suspended. In 1948 Orff was asked to produce the same type of music that had distinguished the Guentherschule, this time for a series of educational broadcasts on Bavarian radio. He revised his educational plan, originally intended for the training of physical education teachers, with a new focus on the needs and abilities of children. The work of his colleague, Gunild Keetman, formerly a student at the Guentherschule, was crucial in the adaptation of the *Schulwerk* to children's levels. The broadcasts continued for five years. Experimental courses with children were begun at the Mozarteum in Salzburg. Soon the Orff *Schulwerk* had become a regular part

of the curriculum there, with Keetman and others as teachers. Salzburg became a headquarters for *Schulwerk,* and its inclusion in the program there was an important step in the spread of the method to other countries. Today the Orff Institute, established in Salzburg in 1963, offers training in the method for teachers from many parts of the world.

Leaders in the dissemination of the *Schulwerk* to other countries were Doreen Hall and Arnold Walter of Canada, Daniel Hellden of Sweden, Minna Ronnefeld of Denmark, and Naohiro Fukui of Japan.

There are several English-language publications that draw significantly on the material in the German edition of *Music for Children.* Among them are the Hall-Walter edition (Canada) and the Margaret Murray edition (Great Britain). The United States edition, edited by Dr. Hermann Regner of the Orff Institute, includes exercises, songs, lesson plans and articles submitted by a number of educators.

The American Orff-*Schulwerk* Association, formed in 1968, has more than four thousand members and publishes a quarterly journal, the *The Orff Echo.* Some teachers have explored the feasibility of combining Orff *Schulwerk* with Kodály's sol-fa teaching. Leaders of each movement have visited and learned from each other, as Wilhelm Keller has pointed out:

> It may be interesting to get a short history of contacts between Hungarian colleagues and co-workers of Kodaly and the Orff Institute; further to come to know what the difference is between Orff-*Schulwerk* and the "Kodaly method." In the last year of Kodaly's life the Orff Institute was able to establish and foster contact with him and a few of his colleagues—Gabor Friss, Dr. Josef Peter, Dr. Otto Borhy, Isvanna Gaal, Katalin Forrai and others. The first meetings with Hungarian music pedagogues during the annual "Week's Conference on Music Education" in Graz, Austria, in which Dr. Hermann Regner and I took part, followed the ISME Conference in Budapest where I gave a lecture on fundamental music education and its significance as an introduction to modern music. After this lecture I had a dialogue with Zoltán Kodály concerning the Orff-Instruments. Kodály told me that he had bought a collection of Orff-Instruments for a school in a Hungarian town and that he liked the sound of xylophones more than the sound of glockenspiels. In 1965 followed a visit by Dr. Regner and Professor Waldmann of Trossingen to learn about the practice of music teaching according to Kodály's ideas in Budapest.[9]

To be in keeping with the Orff philosophy, each culture must base its *Schulwerk* pedagogy on its own heritage of children's lore. Orff himself seemed to think that the philosophy and most of the techiques could be used in virtually any country. The materials, however, are so closely related to the stories, poems, games, and songs of childhood in a particular culture that to adopt them without change seems inappropriate. Leading *Schulwerk* teachers have studied the principles and the teaching techniques and have then shaped the instructional repertoire from materials that are suitable for a particular nationality. Since Orff made extensive use of songs in the pentatonic mode for the first portion of the course, and this mode was so closely related, in his opinion, to the musical life of the young child, it seems logical to collect indigenous pentatonic songs for use in Orff-inspired teaching. Those with extensive experience in teaching *Schulwerk* suggest that American folk music includes a wealth of pentatonic songs and singing games.

Notes

1. Carl Orff, "Orff-Schulwerk: Past and Future," *Perspectives in Music Education* (Washington, DC: Music Educators National Conference, 1966), 386.

2. Carl Orff, *Documentation: His Life and Works*, vol. 3. Translated by Margaret Murray. (New York: Schott Music Corporation, 1978), 17.

3. Dorothee Guenther, "Elemental Dance," *Orff Institute Year Book 1962* (Mainz: B. Schott's Sohne, 1963), 37.

4. Arnold Walter, "Introduction" to Carl Orff and Gunild Keetman, *Music for Children*, English adaptation by Doreen Hall and Arnold Walter (Mainz: B. Schott's Sohne, 1960).

5. Carl Orff, "Introduction to *Music for Children*."

6. Wilhelm Keller, "What is the Orff-Schulwerk—and What It is Not!" *Musart* 22, No. 5 (April–May 1970), 50.

Carl Orff delivered this paper in a speech at the opening session of an Orff elementary education course at the University of Toronto in the summer of 1962. It was given in German and translated by Arnold Walter of the Faculty of Music of the University. The paper first appeared in the *Canadian Music Educator* and is reprinted here from the April–May 1963 issue of the *Music Educators Journal*.

The *Schulwerk*—Its Origins and Aims

by Carl Orff

The nature of the *Schulwerk*, its aim and purpose, can perhaps best be explained by describing how it came into being. Looking back, I am tempted to call it a wildflower (being a passionate gardener I am given to such comparisons). Just as wildflowers grow wherever they find suitable conditions, so the *Schulwerk* grew and developed, finding nourishment in my work. It was not the result of a preconceived plan—I never would have been able to plan so far ahead—it simply arose from a need which I recognized. We all know from experience that wildflowers thrive in abundance while carefully tended garden flowers disappoint us sometimes; they lack the strength of natural growth.

Such natural growth has advantages and disadvantages. Those who look for a method or a ready-made system are rather uncomfortable with the *Schulwerk;* people with artistic temperament and a flair for improvisation are fascinated by it. They are stimulated by the possibilities inherent in a work which is never quite finished, in flux, constantly developing. It is only natural that such a procedure may be dangerous at times; it may run in the wrong direction. Anyone who wishes to advance on his own, needs a thorough professional training and, in addition, an intimate knowledge of the style of the *Schulwerk*, a grasp of its aim and potential.

Unfortunately, it has often been misinterpreted, exploited, and falsified to the point of caricature. Yet a great amount of material sent to me year after year by truly outstanding teachers—letters, photographs, tapes, articles, reports—has confirmed and endorsed the soundness of my approach. I appreciate their attitude.

To return to its origins: in the twenties the younger generation was captivated by a new feeling for the body, for sport, gymnastics, and dance. Jaques-Dalcroze had helped to prepare the ground for the new movement; his "Institute for Music and Rhythm" in Hellerau became widely known. Rudolf Von Laban and Mary Wigman (to mention only those two) were at the height of their careers. Laban was a magnificent teacher, an outstanding choreographer; his book on the dance earned him great fame. Mary Wigman—a disciple of Dalcroze and Laban and a great star in her own right—created a new expressive dance. The impact of their work was enormous; both teaching and performing were deeply influenced by it. It was a time when numerous schools for gymnastics and dance came into being. Being keenly interested in the whole movement, I added to their number. Together with Dorothea Guenther—she was to become one of the outstanding teachers in her field—I established, in 1924, the Guentherschule in Munich. Uppermost in my mind was the creation of a rhythmic education; also the realization of my main idea that music and movement ought to be taught simultaneously, supplementing one another and intimately connected. How necessary this was I had learned in the theatre. Working with singers, actors, dancers, and musicians, I discovered a surprising lack of rhythmic awareness, a total absence of proper training.

The most remarkable thing about the Guentherschule was probably the fact that one of its founders and directors happened to be a musician. Musical activities were looked upon with favor; I had every opportunity to try out my ideas, to experiment. There was no doubt in my mind that the training had to be totally different from what was customary at that time. The accent was on rhythm. We had to find instruments that lent themselves to this approach. It was my ambition to bring all students to the point where they could accompany their own dances and exercises as competently as musicians would. I did not want to have anything to do with piano accompaniments which were then (and still are) being used in the training of movement. I wanted the students to become musicians in their own right. Wigman's experiments showed me the way; I still remember every detail of her sensational witchdance, accompanied only by African rattles.

Instead of making them play the piano (so out of place in a school of movement and dance) I taught the students instruments that had rhythmical impact, primitive appeal—and were easy to handle. Of course such instruments have first to be found. There was no shortage of percussion straight and simple, whether native or exotic; the current development of jazz had seen to that: we had only to choose what we wanted. An independent ensemble, however, called for melody and bordun instruments. For that reason we proceeded to build rhythm instruments capable of carrying melody—xylophones, metallophones, and glockenspiels in various sizes and forms. Some were new, some influenced by medieval and exotic models. The trogxylophone, for instance, had little in common with the xylophones usually found in orchestras; it was actually a descendant of highly developed Indonesian types. In Karl Maendler, a piano and harpsichord manufacturer of genius, I found a man who was sympathetic to my ideas and willing to experiment. It took him years to develop all those instruments which are taken for granted today; but he succeeded in adding incomparable, irreplaceable timbres to our ensemble. New also were the ranges—there appeared soprano, alto, tenor, and bass models of both xylophones and metallophones. New was a playing technique made possible by the addition of resonance boxes and by the use of soft mallets; the sound became infinitely more variable.

If I may digress for a moment, I would like to mention that these perfected xylophones and metallophones have found their way into our opera and symphony orchestras. I myself use them in quantity in *Antigone* and *Oedipus* (ten to twelve large xylophones) where they dominate the orchestral timbre.

But back to the Guentherschule; the flute soon joined the ensemble as a melody instrument. It is, of course, one of the oldest, one might say a primeval instrument. After experimenting with exotic varieties I decided to use the recorder. Together with harpsichords and gambas it had been rediscovered in the course of the revival of old music. Until then, that is until the first years of our century, recorders had been hidden away in museums. With the help of Curt Sachs, at that time curator of the famous Berlin collection of ancient instruments, I was able to assemble a quartet of recorders built after old models—descant, treble, tenor and bass. How the interest in recorders had suddenly developed can be gleaned from the fact that Fritz Joede started to use them at about the same time in his work with the Youth Movement; but only for the performance of old music.

I still remember the day when we received the very first quartet of recorders in the Guentherschule—I remember our helplessness and confusion; there wasn't anybody who could tell us how to play them. We had to work it out by trial and error, and did so in a completely unhistorical manner. I have always regretted that recorder playing (particularly as practiced in the Youth Movement) became almost a pest, that the instruments fell so soon into ill repute. Mass production of cheap and unreliable models had a great deal to do with it; also the strange belief that anything and everything could be played on them.

For the bass part of our ensemble—sustained fifths and borduns—we used kettledrums, low xylophones, also strings: cellos, fiddles and gambas of all sorts. A group of plucked instruments consisting of lutes and guitars completed our ensemble.

Now music had to be created, composed, or arranged from satisfactory original source material; folk music (both native and foreign) proved very valuable in this respect. In my teaching I tried to bring the students to the point where they could invent music of their own to accompany movement, however modest such inventions might be at first. They grew out of spontaneous improvisations in which a student could freely express himself. Our pieces were not first written out and afterwards performed. They were extemporizations. After much playing some might be set in notation. Reading was rather uncommon; the music was learned by heart and played from memory. At the end we did, of course, write down what we played in order not to forget it, in order also to illustrate our pedagogical intentions. Thus originated the first edition of the *Schulwerk* in 1930. Its first volume began with the statement: "The *Schulwerk* concerns itself with the primary forces and forms of music." In quick succession there appeared additional volumes such as "Playing Percussion and Tambourine," "Playing Kettledrums," "Playing Xylophones," "Playing Recorders," also "Dances and Instrumental Pieces for Various Combinations."

Gunild Keetman, my erstwhile pupil and lifelong assistant, collaborated with me on the development of the instrumental ensemble and on the preparation of the volumes just mentioned. Hans Bergese and Wilhelm Twittenhoff also assisted me in various ways. In due course the Guentherschule boasted an ensemble of dancers with an orchestra of their own. Music and choreography were supervised by Gunild Keetman and Maja Lex, respectively. Dancers and players were interchangeable; it also happened that suitable instruments (flutes, cymbals, drums, etc.) were integrated in the dance itself. To illustrate the diversity and variety of such an orchestra let me list the instruments employed: Recorders, xylophones, the metallophones of all ranges, glockenspiels, kettledrums, small drums, tom-toms, gongs, various kinds of cymbals, triangles, tune bells; sometimes also fiddles, gambas, spinettinos, and portativos. The group toured Germany and other European countries; its performances were invariably successful. In addition the ensemble appeared at teachers' conventions and educational conferences, thereby drawing attention to the *Schulwerk*.

Music educators had taken an interest in my experiments from the beginning. Foremost among them was Leo Kestenberg, most influential at that time because of his position in the Ministry of Education in Berlin.

Assisted by Dr. Preussner and Dr. Walter, he espoused the cause of the *Schulwerk;* in fact he planned to test it on a grand scale in the public schools—a decision that led to immediate publication of the *Schulwerk* material. I still admire the courage of my publisher friends Ludwig and Willy Strecker (owners of Schott in Mainz) in printing it—and that at a time when the instruments called for were still in scant supply. Kestenberg's plan, however, was never put into operation. He soon had to relinquish his position, a political wave sweeping away all of the ideas which we had realized. Whatever was saved from the wreckage was misunderstood and misinterpreted.

During the war the Guentherschule was completely destroyed, the buildings gutted by fire, the instruments lost. It was never rebuilt. Times had changed; I had given up teaching. And yet I expected, subconsciously, a new call.

The call came. It came in 1948. It was quite literally a call—from the Bavarian radio. One of their officials, a Dr. Panofsky, had discovered an out-of-print recording from the time of the Guentherschule and had played it to the director of school programming. The music on the record was scored for the ensemble I have described earlier. What they asked me was this: "Could you write us some music on these lines? Music that children might be able to play by themselves? We think that it would appeal to them. Three or four broadcasts perhaps?"

I was working on the score of *Antigone* at the time and was completely out of touch with educational problems; but I found the offer attractive, it presented a challenge. A challenge indeed! The instruments which had been used in the Guentherschule were gone. Times were bad, raw material unavailable—how would we get new instruments? But that was not all. The old *Schulwerk* had addressed itself to an older age group, to prospective teachers of movement and dance. As it stood it was not applicable to children.

All of a sudden the tragic interruption of my earlier work became meaningful—I saw in a flash where rhythmical education really ought to begin: when a child enters school—or earlier still, at pre-school age. Although my previous experiments were out of date now because of my new insights, my years of experience had prepared me for a fresh start. That the unity of music and movement is still naturally present in the child (adolescents have already lost it, and must relearn it) is so sadly overlooked that it became the cornerstone of my new pedagogical work. I suddenly understood what the first *Schulwerk* had lacked: the singing voice, the word. A child quite naturally starts with a call, a rhyme, with text and tune together; movement, play and song coalesce and integrate. I would never have been able to bring myself to "write a few pieces for children" for radio, seeing how busy I was at that time; but I was fascinated by the idea of a musical education completely geared to the child. So I accepted the offer and went to work, but in my own way.

I began to see things in the right perspective. "Elemental" was the password, applicable to music itself, to the instruments, to forms of speech and movement. What does it mean? The Latin word *elementarius* from which it is derived means "pertaining to the elements, primeval, basic." What, then, is elemental music? Never music alone, but music connected with movement, dance, and speech—not to be listened to, meaningful only in active participation. Elemental music is pre-intellectual, it lacks great form, it contents itself with simple sequential structures, ostinatos, and miniature rondos. It is earthy, natural, almost a physical activity. It can be learned and enjoyed by anyone. It is fitting for children.

Gunild Keetman and I, assisted by an experienced educator, shaped the first broadcasts and started to build the series. We worked with children and for children. The result was the new *Schulwerk*.

Our melodic starting point was the falling minor third. The compass was gradually widened until it reached a pentatonic scale without half tones. Linguistically we started with name calls, counting-out rhymes and the simplest of songs. Here was a world easily accessible to children. I wasn't thinking of especially gifted ones. What I had in mind was the education in the broadest terms, applicable to modestly gifted children and even those with very little talent. I knew from experience that few children are completely unmusical, that almost every child can comprehend and enjoy music. Incompetent teachers too often fail to recognize what is inherent in the child. Such teachers do a great deal of damage.

We began our broadcasts in the Autumn of 1948 with unprepared school children between the ages of eight and twelve using whatever was left of the Guentherschule instruments. The children were fascinated. As they played, their enthusiasm made its mark on the listener. It soon became clear (as I had foreseen) that the short series of broadcasts originally planned was wholly inadequate; that we were at the beginning of a far-reaching development. Where it would lead was impossible to predict. The response from the schools was beyond all expectation. Children were excited, they all wanted to learn to play that kind of music; requests for information mounted, people wanted to know where instruments could be bought. A young pupil of old Maendler, Klauss Becker, came to our assistance. With whatever material he could lay hands on, he put together the first xylophones and metallophones for the new *Schulwerk*. He too was successful. After a year he was able to open a workshop of his own called Studio 49, where our instruments are steadily being improved.

Soon the radio organized competitions for the children who played, as well as for the children who were listening, with instruments as prizes. Rhymes and simple poems had to be set to music; the compositions (both melody and accompaniment) had to be written out. The results were most gratifying and proved to us that the broadcasts had been properly understood and digested.

They lasted five full years and laid the groundwork for five basic volumes which appeared between 1950 and 1954. Their title—Music for Children.

In 1949 Gunild Keetman joined the staff of the Mozarteum in Salzburg to give regular courses in the *Schulwerk*; Dr. Preussner, the Director of the Academy, had known it since his early days with Kestenberg. Here it was possible to pay more attention to movement, an aspect that naturally doesn't lend itself to broadcasting. Demonstrations and performances aroused interest. Delegates to international conferences held at the Mozarteum became acquainted with the *Schulwerk* and decided to make use of it in their own countries. One of them was Arnold Walter, who prevailed upon Doreen Hall to study with Keetman in Salzburg and to introduce the *Schulwerk* into Canada after her return. Daniel Hellden carried it to Sweden, Mina Lange to Denmark. It also found its way to Switzerland, Belgium, Holland, England, Portugal, Yugoslavia, Latin America, Turkey, Israel, Greece and finally Japan. The tapes of the original broadcasts did much to prepare the way. They were rebroadcast by many foreign stations.

All this made it necessary to translate and adapt the German edition. It wasn't simply a question of translation but rather of using a country's folklore, its nursery rhymes and children's songs in the same way as the German poems have been used in the original. Doreen Hall and Arnold Walter prepared the first foreign version; since then the *Schulwerk* has been published in Swedish, Flemish, Danish, English, French, Spanish, and Portuguese, with a Japanese edition in preparation.

After concluding the five volumes of *Music for Children,* two sets of recordings, and a film, I thought that I had come to the end of my pilgrimage. But the growing interest in the *Schulwerk*, the editing just mentioned, the additions of whole new fields, such as music therapy, kept me extremely busy.[1] They still do. Requests for teachers, the discovery also that the *Schulwerk* has all too often been wrongly interpreted convinced me of the need for an authentic training center. Once again it was Dr. Preussner who came to my assistance by creating such a center in the Mozarteum; in this he was generously supported by the Austrian authorities whose help I gratefully acknowledge. The new institute devotes itself exclusively to the *Schulwerk* and, in particular, to the training of teachers. It attracts students from all over the world.

Notes

1. A few months after Orff made his speech, a therapeutical and sociopedagogical research division was to have been added, with Wilhelm Keller in charge.

What is the Orff-*Schulwerk* Approach to Teaching?

By Konnie Saliba

Orff-*Schulwerk* can be described as a pedagogy that organizes the elements of music through speaking, singing, playing and moving. Carl Orff described this approach as an "idea" and as a "wildflower," conveying the thought that with nurturing, a wildflower will flourish and yet maintain its identity. He discussed "elemental" music as music that is spontaneous and near to the earth. He considered elemental music not as performance music that one perfects through technical mastery but as music that is produced at the moment by group participation and design.

A teacher not schooled in the techniques of teaching in the Orff process might logically ask, "What in this method is different from other teaching?" The best way to answer this question is to focus on the elements that make Orff teaching work.

In the Orff approach, experience precedes conceptualization. For example, materials presented to children in the second grade should be in phrase lengths of eight beats, in $\frac{2}{4}$ meter. If the teacher presents this type of phrase consistently in a poem, echo clapping, and movement exercises, the children will come to know this structure internally. In traditional approaches to teaching music, rhythmic and melodic notation are beginning points; the child comes to know about music through a deductive method. Orff-*Schulwerk* is an inductive approach in which multiple experiences in speech, rhythm, singing, moving, and playing are the focus of carefully planned lessons, so that children make and participate in music. The ways in which music is written are introduced in detail when the child needs a means for remembering what he or she has done.

Child Development

In order to know how to teach children, teachers need a thorough knowledge of the nature of children and their capabilities. If, for example, a teacher introduces multiple ostinatos to a class of six-year-olds, the children will not be successful because they are not developmentally ready for this task. If, on the other hand, the teacher introduces instrumental sound exploration in a creative framework, the children will be successful. Likewise, if a ten-year-old is asked to sing a song based on the intimate, small sound of the *sol–mi* interval (the "universal chant" of childhood), the child will be uncomfortable because this is psychologically not appropriate for him or her. In the areas of singing, rhythm, speech, and movement, the teacher must be knowledgeable about appropriate tasks for different ages.

Singing

Singing should be a primary focus for all Orff teachers. The fact that there are instruments should not be an excuse for not developing the singing voice. At kindergarten level, games for tone matching should occur in each lesson. Children should also be able to listen to a melodic pattern the teacher sings and to echo-sing it accurately. These patterns should be presented continually with appropriate folk melodies to expand the students' melodic repertoire. As the children develop, their singing should include using such things as Curwen's hand signals and visualizations of melodies. Children should be exposed to the practice of singing portions of melodies in thirds. Throughout the training of the singing voice, however, the teacher should be aware of the appropriate singing range for children of different ages, and should focus on correct posture, breathing, enunciation, and a clear tone that is free of tension. What may work for one child may not work for another: the creative Orff teacher uses many ways to approach training the singing voice.

Rhythm

In Orff teaching, rhythm is the primary component of musical expression. Children naturally use the body as a means of expressing rhythm. The body can be used in rhythmic ways by clapping, patting, snapping, or stamping. The body can provide accompaniments to rhymes, songs, or games. Alternatively, rhythm can be experienced through movement, superimposed instrumental ostinatos, or instrumental accompaniments on Orff percussion instruments.

Harmony

The beginning accompaniment, and one of the mainstays of Orff-*Schulwerk*, is the *bordun*, an accompaniment based on the first and fifth scale degrees. (For example, in the key of F the bordun is F and C). The open fifth is a childlike sound, and as a single harmony accompaniment, easy for even the youngest child to perform.

A bordun can be used with all melodies based upon a whole tone pentatonic scale (*do-re-mi-so-la*). The bordun, played beneath the melody, provides an appropriate and elemental background for singing. The technique of the bordun, which may have preceded polyphony in the sequence of music history, is elemental and unsophisticated in sound. From the bordun comes harmonic parallelism.

Later in the sequence of instruction, the harmony includes descants and eventually traditional I-V and I-IV-V harmonizations.

Form

Form is the most important element in group music making: it is the structure that gives cohesion to Orff teaching. A basic principal of Orff teaching is that a totality must be presented. This totality might be the singing of a melody or speaking a rhyme or proverb in its entirety. The teacher could present the material verbally (rote) or use a visual for the words or melody, or both. In teaching from the totality, the teacher should do the entire selection once for the class, giving all the children a general impression. From this point, the skill of the teacher comes to the forefront. A creative teacher will recognize different ways to teach the material, enabling each child to gain confidence in mastering any difficulties. Eventually the teacher should combine phrases, returning to the total selection. This is what is referred to as the "Orff process." If instruments are to be used, all children are taught to play the parts first using body percussion. This is to assure that everyone has mastered the technique and not just the talented few. Last of all, the form is introduced by the teacher, or ideas for the form are solicited from the children.

If this segment of the lesson were a poem, the form might be: A—poem, with vocal inflection and body percussion ostinato; A1—the rhythm of the poem, transferred to unpitched percussion instruments; A—poem with body percussion ostinato.

Sound Color

The Orff instruments can be used like any educational instruments, but they have the advantage of producing an extremely poetic world of sound. As an instrumentarium (integrated ensemble) of drums, rattles, woods, xylophones, glockenspiels and metallophones, they possess an extraordinary timbral range. They can be used to provide a soft background; a rich accompaniment; a powerful, ritualistic force; or a childlike accompaniment to a simple chant. They are magic in sound, and this does not escape the imagination of the child.

Movement and Locomotion

Children loves to express themselves in movement. A good Orff teacher provides a framework for all kinds of movement and locomotion experiences. The range is wide and includes body percussion training, movement to accompany singing, gestures with the body, creative movement, and, of course, dance. Movement is a visual illustration of musical concepts and an important ingredient in the expression of creativity. Movement should be encouraged and nurtured, from the explorations of the young child, to the presentation of form and structure for the upper elementary student.

Creativity

For the child, it is not enough simply to reproduce music. Each child needs opportunities to express himself or herself in a personal way. Moments for creativity should be incorporated into every lesson. These ways can be as simple as individual creative movement, or providing a sound color background for someone else's creative movement. For older students, creativity extends to the technique of question-answer improvisation, or the creation of a melody for a poem or a story. A good teacher provides the child with a language—the language of music—and the student then finds ways to express himself or herself using this language.

Knowledge

Although we should include joy in our teaching and focus upon cooperation and group activity, we should not neglect knowledge. Good music education must include conscious learning. There are many ways to introduce the theories of rhythm and melody to children, and carefully balanced lessons should reflect this. Upper elementary age children should be able to transfer symbol to sound and sound to symbol.

Universal Appeal

The Orff Instrumentarium was inspired by primitive instruments from Europe (recorders, glockenspiels, Renaissance instruments), Africa (xylophones, drums, and wooden instruments), Asia (metallophones and other metal percussion instruments), and the Americas (jazz percussion, bass, and Latin percussion instruments). The Orff spirit has spread throughout the world because everyone can reproduce his or her own folk music in authentic ways using the Orff percussion instruments.

In the original volumes of Orff-*Schulwerk*, Orff and Gunild Keetman provided the teacher with *models*. The word "model" implies not only an example but the possibility of development, extension, and creativity. The word itself implies a pattern; it might be more clearly defined as a pattern to be adapted. This is the structure of summer training courses for teachers, to provide many models for the teacher to use as points of departure.

This is a beautiful aspect of teaching using the ideas of Orff-*Schulwerk*, but it is also a problem. Some teachers interpret the Orff approach as a system that lacks structure. A precise structure, if defined by step-by-step procedures, could destroy the nurturing of creative elements. Those teachers, however, who think there is no structure are badly misinformed: there is rather a balance between structure and freedom, which must be respected at all times.

The Orff approach appeals to the teacher who does not mind accepting the challenge of trying new ways to reach musical goals. Many teachers, though attracted to the ideas because they see the value of integrating singing, playing, moving, and creating, feel insecure in some areas, particularly in those of movement and creativity. Those who approach the *Schulwerk* one small step at a time will find many initial fears ill-founded. It is the secure teacher who knows that even the best planned lessons are not always perfect. It is the teacher who is willing to take risks and then evaluate lessons carefully who will grow and find Orff-*Schulwerk* a mode for musical growth.

Process and Improvisation in Orff-*Schulwerk*

by Mary Shamrock

The Orff-*Schulwerk* pedagogy can be considered a model or framework for designing learning experiences intended to nurture musicality. It purports to train a general, group-oriented musicality rather than one that is specific and individual; expression and training are accomplished through singing, moving the body, speaking and performing body sound gestures in rhythmic contexts, and playing simple instruments including the barred percussion designed especially for this approach. The *Schulwerk* is concerned with "elemental" music, the basic building blocks, and therefore has upper limits in terms of musical sophistication. But there need be no apologies for these limits—they follow from the intent of the approach, which is to establish a foundation upon which higher levels of musical development can be built.

Two essential and somewhat unique features of the pedagogy itself—beyond obvious characteristics such as the special instruments and the initial use of the pentatonic mode—are the importance given to structuring the learning process and the emphasis upon improvisation. The learning process is of course significant in *any* approach: unless effective learning takes place, there will be no improvement in musical performance and no musical growth. Also, improvisation is often considered an advanced skill, to be developed only after considerable musical foundation has been established. An emphasis, such as that of the Orff approach, on improvisation for young children may seem highly suspect. The following discussion is an attempt to clarify the role and the intent of process and improvisation in the Orff-*Schulwerk* approach.

Process

Perhaps the most common use of the term "process" in Orff-*Schulwerk* is in reference to the sequence of events in a particular lesson, carefully planned by the teacher to lead the students to attain desired goals—for example, the understanding of certain concepts or the skills needed to play specific instrumental parts or to use movement in a particular way. The *Schulwerk* approach considers the experience of music and movement to be primary; any intellectualization, including the reading of notation, must be built upon this experience. Introduction of any new material thus relies upon rote presentation by the teacher rather than reading. The *Schulwerk* also is based upon the play activities of children—structured and purposeful, but also spontaneous and joyful. Thus the task of the teacher is to devise a sequence of events that will lead students gradually toward the intended goal with a sense of confidence, with success at each level, and with a playful, positive attitude. The activities are goal-oriented, but they are also satisfying in their own right.

The accomplishments of a particular day, week, or longer period may be combined into a "product" that is performable for others. Ideally, performance in a *Schulwerk* curriculum will result from interactive classroom learning activity rather than rehearsing and polishing of specially chosen material.

Such a process is used frequently to teach a set piece, which may include its own combination of singing, playing instruments, speech, movement, or other options. The presentation of a multiple-part set piece through such means is indeed intricate; it represents teaching "by rote" at a highly refined level. The piece may have many parts—it may call for singing in unison or parts, instrumentation with several pitched layers enriched with nonpitched timbres including those of body percussion, text presented in free or rhythmic speech, and free or structured movement in space. The teacher prepares the students through imitative exercises for the rhythmic and melodic patterns used in the lesson, gradually builds up (through extension) the actual parts to be learned, and reinforces the parts through creative repetition. A comparable sequence can be followed for movement and other components. Gradually, the teacher and students layer the parts one upon another and combine them to shape the desired total form.

The teacher bears great responsibility for the success of this rote process. He or she needs to know every part perfectly in order to demonstrate them without hesitation and with little or no time wasted in consultation of notation. He or she also must maintain an objective distance in order to observe what the students are actually accomplishing. If difficulty is encountered at any given stage, learning activities must be repeated or new ones devised so that students become secure in performing the problematic material in question. If the students are not successful, more often than not it is because the teacher's presentation has not been sufficiently clear and sequential.

Planning and executing such lessons in refined rote teaching is an excellent discipline. This is especially true for new educators, but it also applies to experienced music teachers. It is a test not only of musical technique but also of communicative and evaluative skills. In the Orff approach the discipline of learning by imitation is crucial for students since this is the primary means for assimilating new material. The final test of the teacher's effectiveness is not only whether the students perform the material correctly but also whether they enjoy it on an artistic and aesthetic level.

Although a very necessary component in the *Schulwerk* approach, this level of process teaching and learning serves only the foundation level of the *Schulwerk*—the ability to recreate. The higher goal is the ability to create, which is begun by developing the ability to improvise. Improvisation here identifies the facility to rearrange known material spontaneously from the very simplest level.

Improvisation

If a child, for example, has sung simple game songs using *mi, re,* and *do,* before long he or she will be able to create little patterns using these three tones for different words and in different arrangements. If the child has reproduced many rhythm patterns in $\frac{4}{4}$ meter with clapping and other body instruments and has used this meter frequently in speech activities, he or she will soon be able to invent short patterns within this rhythmic structure—without the need for an immediate model. First attempts in this direction come in the form of "question and answer" exercises, in which freedom is specifically limited.

Such fledgling improvisational skills are also fostered in movement and in playing instruments. Often everyone is asked to improvise together at first, to lessen possible anxiety in the face of responding alone. The somewhat chaotic sound that results is unimportant; the value lies in each student's discovering possibilities that then may be expressed independently. In the *Schulwerk* approach, each new musical building block added to the conscious layer of musical experience is reinforced through use in improvisation. The skillful teacher can encourage and assist students in shaping and expressing their ideas and in gaining confidence in this area.

Improvisation on a larger scale has a place in the use of repertoire. Orff-*Schulwerk* repertoire—the song arrangements, choral speech pieces, instrumental pieces, movement designs, and so on, that are found in the original *Schulwerk* volumes and the many publications appearing since their publication—must be viewed from two perspectives. Many are delightful as musical entities and are worthy of performance in the traditional sense of that word. Treating them as performance pieces has a place within the overall scheme: that practice fosters learning technical aspects of playing, becoming familiar with a new musical element such as a mode or meter, learning the sound of effective texture and timbre combinations, providing ready-made music for an experience focusing on dance or drama, providing the basis for an expanded form, and more.

Consistent with the intent of the *Schulwerk* pedagogy, however, published repertoire is also viewed as a framework for the development and extension of learning experiences. Given that certain items lend themselves better to a particular age group or ability level, it can be said generally that it is more appropriate to modify material to suit the needs of the students using it than to search out material that the students will be able to perform. Possibilities for modification are infinite: parts may be simplified, textures made thicker or thinner, vocal parts played on instruments and vice versa, texts presented as speech only, sections repeated with different instrumentation, completely new sections added featuring improvisation, and so on. The skilled teacher very soon draws the students into helping devise these modifications, and it is through such participation that children learn to evaluate the relative success of each attempt and lay the foundation for creating their own original pieces using similar techniques.

The transition from spontaneous improvisation (for its own sake or as a contrasting section in a set piece) to the creation of new compositions comes when particularly successful rhythmic, melodic, or spatial improvisations are purposely remembered and then expanded into small forms. The need for remembering provides an immediate setting for learning the basics of music notation. In the *Schulwerk* approach, this may be done by whatever means the teacher wishes; many have elected to employ solfège, hand signs, and various other techniques drawn from other approaches. The extent of the group creative efforts really knows no limits except the time and facilities available. As individuals contribute ideas and effort, small forms expand into larger forms, complete with movement, dramatic content, special costumes, scenery, and so on—and all with the immeasurable satisfaction that comes with creating something independent and new.

Product

The term "process" in the broader sense of the Orff pedagogy must embrace this development of independent creative facility. Guiding this process is indeed a challenge with inherent risks. Once the students are given responsibility for developing their own material, results are no longer predictable. The teacher must remain open to different interpretations of what may seem to be very clear-cut tasks, while the tendency to accept only results that conform to the teacher's norm is difficult to overcome. Since students will vary in their natural creative tendencies, the teacher must guard against allowing the most talented to flourish at the expense of the less gifted. Fortunately, the *Schulwerk*, because of its many dimensions, provides opportunity for virtually all students to contribute according to their strengths. The more independent the students become, the more the teacher becomes a consultant rather than an instructor. There never ceases, however, to be a point at which new material and new possibilities are not appropriate and indeed necessary; a balance must be struck between cultivating the students' newfound creative abilities and incorporating new movement and musical elements.

The ideal product of the *Schulwerk* process is a student who can function as a musician on an elemental level as both performer and creator and who has the ability to self-evaluate both roles. The transition from the imitative to the creative level is accomplished through the development of skills in improvising. The teacher serves as instructor, model, motivator, evaluator, and facilitator, increasingly relinquishing these roles to the students as they gain the ability to assume them. Given the creative dimension, there will be considerable variation in the actual implementation of the *Schulwerk* process and as much variation in the types of creative output.

The highest potential of the approach remains: its potential for awakening and extending the creative capacity of the human being. Without this dimension, the *Schulwerk* approach offers little more than an attractive alternative for group musical performance. It is the *Schulwerk* "process," in the full meaning of the term, that makes possible the fulfillment of this potential.

Arnold Walter was one of the translators of the English edition of Carl Orff's *Music for Children*. The article is reprinted from the January 1959 edition of *The Instrumentalist*.

Carl Orff's
Music for Children

by Arnold Walter

A quarter of a century ago I attended a recital given by students of a school of modern dance—a recital I have never forgotten; it is as clear in my memory as if it had happened yesterday. The place was Munich; the school called itself "Guntherschule;" movement and dance were strongly influenced by Mary Wigman, with an accent on improvisation, but what captivated me completely was the coordination of music and movement, the fact (unique in my experience) that the students were uncommonly well trained in both disciplines.

These students made their own music, now dancing, now playing with equal grace and competence; the whole performance looked and sounded as if it had been improvised on the spot. Dancers would stop dancing to take their place in the "orchestra;" musicians would leave their instruments to join the dancers singly or in groups; sound and motion seemed to be created by the same impulses. One couldn't help feeling that something was coming to life here which had long been forgotten in our civilization: the primeval power, the magic effect of music which "moves" us quite literally—which makes us move and dance as the Greeks did and as the Orient still does today. And one wished that all young musicians could have the privilege of such training, acquiring the rhythmical awareness and melodic imagination of those dancers improvising on flutes and drums.

For the "orchestra" wasn't the usual combination of strings, woodwinds and brasses; it consisted of recorders, viols, bells, glockenspiels, xylophones, and every known kind of drum; small portative organs were on one end of the scale, double-headed Indian drums on the other. The instruments on the stage looked like a page from a medieval manuscript. The music itself had an archaic flavor reminding one of trouvères, jongleurs, and Italian dances of the fourteenth century; but it had also a very modern one bringing Stravinsky to mind, particularly the Stravinsky of *Les Noces*. The reasons were obvious: rhythm was the predominating element; melody grew out of rhythm as it were; drones and ostinati formed the accompaniment; harmony, if used at all, restricted itself to parallel motion resulting in organum-like effects.

No doubt this was a very unusual kind of music. It had the appeal of primitive strength, and yet it was curiously satisfying to modern ears; it didn't accompany the dance, it created it; and it seemed an ideal medium to teach young people what music was all about—to teach them how to respond to it wholly, with every muscle and nerve, with body and soul. The man responsible for the recital was Carl Orff, in those days the musical director of the Guntherschule. Today he is very famous; his operas and scenic oratorios are performed and recorded everywhere. It is sufficient to mention the *Carmina Burana, Der Mond,* and *Antigone;* but however well known as a composer, he is equally famous as a music educator. He had the happy inspiration to teach children the same way he had taught these fascinating dancers, with quite astonishing results.

The pedagogical value of his approach was recognized at once. Radio Munich made use of it in countless broadcasts; and Schott in Mainz published a manual called *Music for Children* (Das Schulwerk) which is in the process of being translated into Turkish and Japanese (it is already available in many European languages); Orff's influence on modern music education is without parallel.

Orff's Pedagogical Approach

What made it so? Orff starts with the premise (learned from ethnomusicology) that the musical development of children roughly corresponds to the growth of music history; rhythm precedes (and is stronger than) melody; melody precedes (and is stronger than) harmony. If you take a child, if you sit him down at the piano, tell him where middle C is and proceed to teach him the "Minuet in G," you introduce him to rhythm, melody, harmony and instrumental technique at one and the same time. He might survive it, certainly; but the chances are that he will learn the piece mechanically, without feeling for rhythm, without enthusiasm for the very polite (and most un-childlike) melody, without appreciation of functional harmony.

A teacher following Orff's precepts will do exactly the opposite. He will start with speech patterns, using single words, phrases or nursery rhymes to illustrate the various types of measure which are experienced rather than explained. Such rhythmical formulas are reproduced by stamping, clapping, and finally on instruments. That is all very primitive and elementary, but that is precisely what it ought to be: elementary, basic. A child finding it difficult to grasp a rhythmical pattern or to hold his own in a rhythmic canon has no business playing the "Minuet in G."

Melodic Materials

Melody is made to grow out of rhythm—imperceptibly, slowly; it is treated with infinite care. Two notes are introduced at first, then three and four, finally five; there is great emphasis on pentatonic tunes, for a variety of reasons. They do not depend on accompaniment, they don't imply harmony, they are the best possible material for improvisation (the technique of Javanese gamelan orchestras proves the point). They are also very beautiful; does anyone know a really bad pentatonic tune?

Major and minor melodies are introduced in due course, but as a final stage in a carefully planned development. And it is precisely that development, the gradual widening-out of the tonal space in the child's mind which is the governing idea of the whole approach. Cadential harmony is treated in a similar way, not as a starting point but as a goal to be reached; familiar chord progressions are preceded by drones, ostinati, and parallel motion.

Use of Instruments

Rhythm patterns, melodies, and ostinato figures are tried out and played on the instruments mentioned earlier. These instruments are anything but toys; they are carefully selected and contrasted, they are in fact replicas of medieval ensembles, as meaningful to children now as they were to grown-up people in those days. They are difficult enough to be a challenge to a child yet simple enough to make improvisation possible. And that is what Orff wants more than anything else—*to enable children to improvise, to invent their own rhythms, melodies, and accompanying figures.* It is a well-known fact that younger children appear often more gifted than older ones: their fertile curiosity, their spontaneous reactions have not been stifled yet by ready-made learning which psychologists recognize as a form of "adult pressure." Such pressure can be avoided only by making the greatest possible use of a child's creative ability. Beauty (says Jean Piaget) is of value only when recreated by those who discover it.

A Truly Creative Approach

It seems that much of our teachings can be summed up in the phrase just quoted: "ready-made learning." The child repeats what he has been taught without discovering music by recreating it. But it is not easy to avoid the traditional ways and means of teaching. It means avoiding all the systems, methods, and primers on the market; avoiding the usual fare of children's songs and easy pieces—avoiding even major modes and functional harmony, to start with at least. And it would be a mistake to think that Orff's book contains a ready-made system to be taught chapter by chapter; it is not that kind of book at all. It points in the right direction but the road to be traveled must be discovered by the teacher himself. Such a teacher must be capable of molding musical material without help from printed pages; he must deal with rhythm, melody, and harmony as painters deal with colors and sculptors with clay—he must be able to encourage children to play with sound objects, to form them, to "compose" them. Which presupposes of course that he can do all that himself.

Is that too much to be asked of a music teacher? Is there any reason why music teachers could not do what art teachers have done so successfully in recent years? Carl Orff certainly blazed a trail which will be followed by many. He realized that there is music in children; but he realized also that it is fundamentally different from the music they would want to learn later on—that it was necessary to breach the gap, not by ready-made learning but by traversing the various stages of music's own growth. That sounds simple. But all great discoveries have an air of simplicity—once they have been made.

References

Dalcroze

Books

Aronoff, Frances Webber. *Music and Young Children*. New York: Holt, Rinehart & Winston, 1969.

Brown, Margaret, and Betty K. Sommer. *Movement Education: Its Evolution and a Modern Approach*. Reading, Massachusetts: Addison-Wesley Publishing Co., 1969.

Chosky, Lois, Robert M. Abramson, Avon E. Gillespie, and David Woods. *Teaching Music in the Twentieth Century*. Englewood Cliffs, NJ: Prentice Hall, 1986.

Driver, Ann. *Music and Movement*. London: Oxford University Press, 1936.

Driver, Ethel. *A Pathway to Dalcroze Eurhythmics*. 1951. Reprint. London: Thomas Nelson and Sons, 1963.

Findlay, Elsa. *Rhythm and Movement: Applications of Dalcroze Eurhythmics*. Evanston, Illinois: Summy-Birchard, 1971.

Gell, Heather. *Music, Movement and the Young Child*. Sydney: Australasian Publishing Company, 1949.

Jaques-Dalcroze, Emile. *Eurhythmics, Art and Education*. Trans. Frederick Rothwell, ed. Cynthia Fox. 1930. Reprint. New York: B. Blom, 1972.

_____. *Eurhythmics, Art and Education*. Arno Press, 1976.

_____. *Rhythmic Movement*. 2 vols. London: Novello and Co., 1920–1921.

_____. *Rhythm, Music and Education*. Trans. Harold F. Rubinstein. Abridged reprint edition. London & Whitstable: The Riverside Press, 1967.

Moog, H. *The Musical Experience of the Pre-school Child*. Trans. C. Clarke. London: Schott, 1976.

Pennington, Jo. *The Importance of Being Rhythmic: A Study of the Principles of Dalcroze Eurhythmics Applied to General Education and to the Arts of Music, Dancing, and Acting*. Based on and adapted from *Rhythm, Music and Education* by Emile Jaques-Dalcroze; with an introduction by Walter Damrosch. New York: G. P. Putnam's Sons, 1925.

Rosenstrauch, Henrietta. *Percussion, Movement and the Child*. Far Rockaway, New York: Carl Van Roy Co., 1964.

Sadler, M. E., ed. *The Eurhythmics of Jaques-Dalcroze*. Boston: Small, Maynard, 1913.

Articles and Studies

Anderson, William M. "East Meets West With Dalcroze Techniques." *Music Educators Journal* 70, no.4 (December 1983), 52–55.

Aronoff, Frances W. "Games Teachers Play: Dalcroze Eurythmics." *Music Educators Journal* 57, no. 6 (February 1971), 28–32.

Baker, M. "Bibliography: Books on Eurhythmics and Some Music." *Etude* 65 (October 1947), 544.

Becknell, Arthur F. "A History of the Development of Dalcroze Eurhythmics in the United States and Its Influence on the Public School Music Program." Doctoral diss., University of Michigan, 1970.

Barr, G. "Rhythm and the Child." *School Arts* 44 (February 1945), 192–195.

Berlin-Papish, T. "Some Uses of the Dalcroze Method in Piano Teaching." *Piano Teacher* 7 (May 1965), 8–11.

Boepple, Paul. "The Study of Rhythm." *Yearbook of the Music Supervisors National Conference* (1931), 192–94.

Brody, Viola A. "The Role of Body-Awareness in the Emergence of Musical Ability." *Journal of Research in Music Education* 1 (Spring 1953), 17.

Campbell, Patricia Shehan. "The Childsong Genre: A Comparison of Songs by and for Children." *Update* 7, no. 3 (1989), 18–20.

Carlson, Deborah Lynn. "Space, Time, and Force: Movement as a Challenge to Understanding Music." *Music Educators Journal* 67, no. 1 (September 1980), 52–56.

Clarke, U. "Dalcroze: Rhythm in a Chain Reaction," *Musical America* 70 (November 15, 1950), 25.

Dobbs, Jack. "Some Great Music Educators: Emile Jaques-Dalcroze." *Music Teacher* 47, no. 8 (August 1968).

Gherkens, Karl W. "Why Not Eurhythmics?" *Etude* 72 (May 1954), 22.

Glenn, Mabelle. "Demonstration of Creative Rhythm." *Yearbook of the Music Supervisors National Conference* (1932), 311–14.

_____. "Trends in Music Education." *Yearbook of the Music Supervisors National Conference* (1933), 258–62.

Grentzer, Rose Marie. "Eurhythmics in the Elementary School Program." *Etude* 62 (January 1944), 22.

Hall, Lucy Duncan. "The Value of Eurhythmics in Education." *Yearbook of the Music Educators National Conference* (1936), 150–53.

Jaques-Dalcroze, Emile. "The Child and the Pianoforte." Trans. F. Rothwell. *Musical Quarterly* 14 (April 1928), 203–15.

_____. "Dalcroze Explains His Method." *Literary Digest* 78 (September 1923), 31–32, 368.

_____. "Eurhythmics and Its Implications." Trans. Frederic Rothwell, *Musical Quarterly* 16 (July 1930), 358.

_____. "Teaching Music Through Feeling." *Etude* 39 (June 1921).

Joseph, Annabelle S. "A Dalcroze Approach to Music Learning in Kindergarten." Doctoral diss., Carnegie-Mellon University, 1982.

Kestenberg, Leo. "Music Education Goes Its Own Way." *Musical Quarterly* 25 (October 1939), 447–48.

Maier, Guy. "The Teacher's Round Table." *Etude* (May 1941), 310.

Martin, Frank. "Eurhythmics: The Jaques-Dalcroze Method." *Music in Education*. International Conference on the Role and Place of Music in the Education of Youth and Adults (Brussels, June 29–July 9, 1953). Soleure, Switzerland: UNESCO, 1955.

Mead, Virginia Hoge. "More Than Mere Movement: Dalcroze Eurhythmics." *Music Educators Journal* 72, no. 6 (February 1986), 42–46.

Mendel, A. "Mental and Bodily Rhythm." *Nation* 134 (February 17, 1932), 210.

Naumberg, M. "The Dalcroze Idea: What Eurhythmics Is and What It Means." *Outlook* 106 (January 17, 1914), 127–31.

Prim, F. M. "The Importance of Girls' Singing Games in Music and Motor Education." *Canadian Music Educator* 30, no. 2 (May 1989), 115–123.

Rosentrauch, Henrietta. "Rhythmic Problems in Music Teaching," *Volume of Proceedings of the Music Teachers National Association* (1946), 342–49.

Scholl, Sharon. "Music for Dancers," *Music Educators Journal* 52 (February–March 1966), 99–102.

Schuster, Hilda M. *Dalcroze Eurhythmics.* Master's thesis, Duquesne University School of Music, 1938.

_____. "Dalcroze Exceptions: Reply to U. Clarke," *Musical America* 70 (December 15, 1950), 12.

Organizations

The Dalcroze Society of America. Marta Sanchez, Director of the Training Center, Carnegie-Mellon University, Pittsburgh, PA 15213

Institut Jaques-Dalcroze. M. Dominique Porte, Directeur, 44 Rue de la Terrassière, Geneva, Switzerland 1206

Kodály

Books

Adam, Jeno. *Growing in Music with Movable Do.* Edited by Georgiana Peterson; trans. Louis Boros, Joseph Held, and Louis Munkachy. Copyright 1971 by Louis Boros, 359D Crowells Park, Highland Park, New Jersey 08904.

Bacon, Denise. *50 Easy Two-Part Exercises: First Steps in A Cappella Part Singing*. Hackensack, NJ: Joseph Boonin, 1977.

_____. *45 Two-Part American Folk Songs for Elementary Grades*. Wellesley, MA: Kodály Musical Training Institute, 1973.

_____. *Let's Sing Together: Songs for 3, 4, and 5 Year Olds from Mother Goose and Others Set to Music According to the Kodály Concept*. Wellesley, Massachusetts: Kodály Musical Training Institute, 1971.

_____. *185 Unison Pentatonic Exercises. First Steps in Sight Singing According to the Kodály Concept*. West Newton, MA: Kodály Center of America, 1977.

Choksy, Lois. *The Kodály Context: Creating an Environment for Musical Learning*. Englewood Cliffs, NJ: Prentice Hall, 1981.

Choksy, Lois. *The Kodály Method*. 2d ed. Englewood Cliffs, NJ: Prentice Hall, 1988.

Choksy, Lois, Robert M. Abramson, Avon E. Gillespie, and David Woods. *Teaching Music in the Twentieth Century*. Englewood Cliffs, NJ: Prentice Hall, 1986.

Daniel, Katinka. *Kodály in Kindergarten: 50 Lesson Plans, Curriculum, Song Collection*. Champaign, IL: Mark Foster Music Co., 1981.

_____. *The Kodály Approach: Method Book 2, Song Collection*. Champaign, IL: Mark Foster Music Co., 1982.

Eosze, Laszlo. *Kodály: His Life in Pictures*. Boston: Crescendo Publishing Co., 1972.

_____. *Zoltan Kodály: His Life and Work*. London: Collet's, 1962; Millville, N.Y.: Belwin Mills, 1972.

Erdei, Peter. *150 American Folk Songs to Sing, Read and Play*. New York: Boosey and Hawkes, 1974.

Erdely, Stephen. *Methods and Principles of Hungarian Ethnomusicology*. Bloomington, Indiana: Indiana University Publications.

Knighton, Keith B. *Ta Bones and Ti Bones: Early Steps in Sight Reading Based on American Folk Material for Use with the Kodály Concept*. Wellesley, MA: Kodály Musical Training Institute, 1976.

Kodály, Zoltán. *Choral Method*. London: Boosey and Hawkes, 1969.

_____. *Visszatekintes*. Ed. Ferenc Bonis, 2 vols. Budapest: Zenemukiado Vallalet, 1964.

Lasczo, Zoltán. *The First Measurement of the Effectiveness of the Kodály Concept in Hungary Using the Seashore Test*. Urbana, IL: CRME, Spring, 1987.

Rabiere-Raverlat, Jacqueline. *Musical Education in Hungary*. Trans. Margaret Safranek. Paris: A. Leduc, 1971.

Sandor, Frigyes. *Musical Education in Hungary*. 2d. ed., revised. Budapest: Corvina, 1969.

Stone, Margaret L. "Kodály and Orff Music Teaching Techniques: History and Present Practice." (Doctoral diss., Kent State University.) Ann Arbor, MI: University Microfilms, 1971.

Szabo, Helga. *The Kodály Concept of Music Education.* English edition by Geoffry Russell-Smith. London: Boosey & Hawkes, 1969. Textbook with 3 LP records.

Szonyi, Erzsebet. *Kodály and Orff Music Teaching Techniques: History and Present Practice.* Doctoral diss., Ann Arbor, MI: University Microfilms, 1971.

_____. *Musical Reading and Writing.* Three volumes. New York: Boosey and Hawkes, 1974–1979.

Vajda, Cecilia. *The Kodály Way to Music: The Method Adapted for British Schools.* London: Boosey and Hawkes, 1974.

Wheeler, Lawrence, and Lois Raebeck. *Orff and Kodály Adapted for the Elementary School.* Dubuque, IA: William C. Brown, 1985.

Young, Percy M. *Zoltan Kodály, A Hungarian Musician.* London: Ernest Benn, 1964.

Zemke, Sister Lorna. *The Kodály Concept: Its History, Philosophy and Development.* Champaign, IL: Mark Foster Music Company, 1974.

Articles and Studies

Adam, Jeno. "The Influence of Folk Music on Public Musical Education in Hungary." *Studia Musicologica* 7 (1965), 10–18.

Bacon, Denise. "Can the Kodály Method Be Successfully Adapted Here?" *Musart* 22, No. 5 (April–May 1970), 14–15.

_____. "Hungary Will Never Outgrow Kodály." *Music Educators Journal* 65, no. 1 (September 1978), 39–44.

_____. "The Why of Kodály." *Music Journal* 29, no. 7 (September 1971), 26.

Borszormenyi-Nagy, Bela. "The Kodály Legacy." *Clavier* 7 (September 1968), 16–17.

Daniel, Katinka. "The Kodály Method." *Clavier* 7 (September 1968), 20–21.

Darazs, Arpad. "The Kodály Method for Choral Training." *American Choral Review* 8, no. 3 (1966), 8–12.

DiBonaventura, M. "Zoltan Kodály: Man and Mountain." *Pan Pipes* 58, no. 3 (1966), 15–16. Also in *Council for Research in Music Education Bulletin* no. 8 (Fall 1966), 59.

Edwards, L. "Hungary's Musical Powerline to the Young." *Music Educators Journal* 57, no. 6 (February 1971), 38.

Hoffer, Charles R. "The Big KO." *Music Educators Journal* 67, No. 6 (February 1981), 46–47.

Kodály, Zoltán. "Folk Song in Pedagogy." *Music Educators Journal* 53, no. 7 (March 1967), 59–61.

Kokas, Klara. "Psychological Testing in Hungarian Music Education." *Journal of Research in Music Education* 17 (Spring 1969), 125–34.

Palotai, Michael. "Has Hungary Outgrown Kodály?" *Music Educators Journal* 64, no. 6 (February 1978), 40–45.

Rappaport, Jonathan C. "Kodály Legacy: Performers Teach—Teachers Perform." *Music Educators Journal* 72, no. 2 (October 1985), 50–52.

Ringer, A.L. "Lives of Kodály." *Saturday Review* (July 31, 1962), 33–34.

Russell-Smith, Geoffry. "Introducing Kodály Principles into Elementary Teaching." *Music Educators Journal* 54, no. 3 (November 1967), 44.

Steen, Phillip L. "Zoltan Kodály's Choral Music for Children and Youth Choirs." Doctoral diss., University of Michigan, 1970.

Szabolsci, Bence. "Kodály and Universal Education." *Studia Musicologica* 3 (1962), 7–9.

Szonyi, Erzsebet. "Zoltan Kodály's Pedagogic Activities." *International Music Educator* (March 1966), 418–420.

Young, Percy M. "Zoltan Kodály—Pioneer in Music Education." *Clavier* 6, no. 4 (1967), 58.

Zemke, Sister Lorna. "A Comparison of the Effects of a Kodály-Adapted Music Instruction Sequence and a More Typical Sequence on Auditory Musical Achievement in Fourth Grade Students." Doctoral diss., University of Southern California, 1970.

Zinar, Ruth. "John Curwen: Teaching the Tonic Sol-Fa Method 1816–1880." *Music Educators Journal* 70, no. 2 (October 1983), 46–47.

Associations

Organization of American Kodály Educators. Dr. James Fields, Executive Secretary, Nicholls State University, Thibodaux, LA 70310

International Kodály Society. Budapest, PO Box 8, H-1502, Hungary

Orff

Books

Bisgaard, Erling and Gulle Stehouwer. *Musicbook O*. Edited and adapted by Tosse Aaron. St. Louis, MO: Magnamusic/Edition Wilhelm, 1976.

Bitcon, Carol Hampton. *Alike and Different: The Clinical and Educational Uses of Orff-Schulwerk*. Santa Ana, CA: Roscha Press, 1976.

Boshkoff, Ruth. *All Around the Buttercup; Early Experiences with Orff Schulwerk*. New York: Schott Music Corporation, 1984.

Brocklehurst, Brian. *Pentatonic Song Book*. London: Schott & Co., n.d.

_____. *Second Pentatonic Song Book*. London: Schott & Co., 1976.

Carley, Isabel, ed. *Orff Re-echoes. Volume 1.* Cleveland Heights, OH: American Orff-Schulwerk Association, 1977.

_____. *Orff Re-echoes. Volume 2.* Cleveland Heights, OH: American Orff-Schulwerk Association, 1985.

Choksy, Lois, Robert M. Abramson, Avon E. Gillespie, and David Woods. *Teaching Music in the Twentieth Century.* Englewood Cliffs, NJ: Prentice Hall, 1986.

Frazee, Jane, with Kent Kreuter. *Discovering Orff: A Curriculum for Music Teachers.* New York: Schott Music Corporation, 1987.

Gagne, Danai, and Judith Thomas. *Dramas in Elemental Scales: A Collection of Mini-Dramas for Voice and Orff Instruments.* St. Louis, MO: Magnamusic Baton, 1983.

Haselbach, Barbara. *Improvisation, Dance, Movement.* Trans. Margaret Murray. St. Louis, MO: Magnamusic-Baton, 1981. (Original edition Stuttgart: Ernst Klett, 1976.)

Hall, Doreen. *Music for Children: Teacher's Manual.* (To accompany Carl Orff and Gunild Keetman's *Music for Children.*) Mainz, Federal Republic of Germany: B. Schott's Sohne, 1960.

Keetman, Gunild. *Elementaria: First Acquaintance with Orff-Schulwerk* London: Schott and Co., Ltd., 1970.

Keller, Wilhelm. *Introduction to Music for Children.* New York: Schott Music Corporation, 1973.

Liess, Andreas. *Carl Orff.* Trans. Adelheide and Herbert Parkin. New York: St. Martin's Press, 1966.

Murray, Margaret, trans. *Carl Orff: His Life and Works.* New York: Schott Music Corporation, 1978.

Orff-Institute Year Books. Mainz, Germany: B. Schott's Sohne, 1962, 1963, 1964–1968.

The Orff Echo: Official Bulletin of the American Orff-Schulwerk Association, ed. Isabel Carley. Cleveland Heights, OH: American Orff-Schulwerk Association.

Orff, Carl, and Gunild Keetman. *Music for Children.* English adaptation by Doreen Hall and Arnold Walter. New York: Associated Music Publishers, 1956.

Orff, Gertrud. *The Orff Music Therapy: Active Furthering of the Development of the Child.* New York: Schott Music Corporation, 1980.

Regner, Hermann. *Music for Children: Orff-Schulwerk American Edition.* New York: Schott Music Corporation, vol. 1, 1972; vol. 2, 1977, vol. 3, 1980.

Stone, Margaret L. "Kodály and Orff Music Teaching Techniques: History and Present Practice." Doctoral diss., Kent State University. Ann Arbor, MI: University Microfilms, 1971.

Szonyi, Erzsebet. *Kodály and Orff Music Teaching Techniques: History and*

Present Practice. Doctoral diss., Ann Arbor, MI: University Microfilms, 1971.

Thomas, Werner, et al. *Carl Orff: A Report in Words and Pictures.* Mainz, Germany: B. Schott's Sohne, 1955.

Wheeler, Lawrence, and Lois Raebeck. *Orff and Kodály Adapted for the Elementary School.* Dubuque, IA: William C. Brown, 1985.

Articles and Studies

Bacon, Denise. "On Using Orff with Kodály." *Musart* 21 (April–May 1969), 45.

Banks, Susan. "Orff-Schulwerk Teaches Musical Responsiveness." *Music Educators Journal* 68, no. 7 (March 1982), 42–43.

Bates, K. "Creative Music with First Year Juniors." *Orff-Schulwerk Society Bulletin* no. 4 (June 1965).

Breuer, Robert. "The Magic World of Carl Orff." *Music Journal* 15 (March 1957), 56.

Burkart, Arnold. "Orff-Schulwerk in Our Schools: Toward a Pedagogical Construct." *Indiana Musicator* (January 1969).

Caddock, DeWayne G. "The Preschooler Discovers Music." *The Orff Echo* 2 (June 1970), 1.

Carley, Isabel. "Music with a Difference." *The Orff Echo* 1 (June 1969), 3.

Castren, David. "Orff and Junior High Percussion." *The Orff Echo* 1 (June 1969), 7.

Daniel, O. "the New German Music—1959" *Saturday Review* 42 (June 27, 1959), 38.

Danziger, Harris. "Orff Brings Theories to Canada." *New York Times* (August 12, 1962).

_____. "Body and Song." *Opera News* 32 (January 13, 1968), 8.

Ferguson, Nancy. "Orff with the Perceptually Handicapped Child." *The Orff Echo* 2 (June 1970), 1.

Frank, Paul L. "Improvisation as a Teaching Device." *Triad* (January 1962).

Guenther, Dorothee. "Elemental Dance." *Orff Institute Year Book 1962.* Mainz, Federal Republic of Germany: B. Schott's Sohne, 1963, 37.

Hamm, Ruth Pollock. "The Challenge of the Orff Approach for Elementary Music Education." *Musart* 22, no. 5 (April–May 1970), 16–17.

Helm, Everett. "Carl Orff." *The Musical Quarterly* 41 (July 1955), 285.

Hoffer, Charles R. "The Big KO." *Music Educators Journal* 67, no. 6 (February 1981): 46–47.

Keller, Wilhelm. "What is the Orff-Schulwerk—and What It is Not!" *Musart* 22, No. 5 (April–May 1970), 20, 49–50.

Nash, Grace C. "Kodály and Orff." *Clavier* 7 (September 1968), 18.

_____. "Music in the Elementary Classroom." *Musart* 22, No. 5 (April–May

1970), 39, 51–52.

_____. "The New Music for Musicality." *Musart* 18 (November–December 1966).

_____. "Orff." The Instrumentalist 19 (December 1967), 2.

Nichols, Elizabeth. "Adapting Orff to the Music Series." *The Orff Echo* 2 (February 1970), 2.

_____. "Music for the Deaf." *The Orff Echo* 1 (June 1969), 4.

_____. "Orff Can Work in Every Classroom." *Music Educators Journal* 57 (September 1970), 43.

Orff, Carl. "Orff-Schulwerk: Past and Future." *Perspectives in Music Education*. Washington, DC: Music Educators National Conference, 1966.

Peterson, A. Viola. "Orff and Kodály Influences in Music Education." *The Rimer* 1, no. 1 (October 1968), 11–12.

Pleasants, Henry. "The Orff Hypothesis." *High Fidelity Magazine* 6 (October 1956), 68.

——. "The Emergence of Orff." *Saturday Review* 36 (September 26, 1953), 68.

Ponath, Louise, and Carol H. Bitcon. "A Behavioral Analysis of Orff-Schulwerk." *Journal of Music Therapy* 9 (Summer 1972), 56–63.

Shamrock, Mary. "Orff Schulwerk: An Integrated Foundation." *Music Educators Journal* 72, no. 6 (February 1986), 51–55.

Schmidt, Lloyd. "Project Orff: Music for Retarded Children, Project Report 1970–1971." Hartford: Connecticut State Department of Education, 1971.

Steinberg, Carl M. "Master-Class Session for the Music Makers of Tomorrow." *High Fidelity Magazine* 9 (June 1959).

Walter, Arnold. "Elementary Music Education: the European Approach." *Canadian Music Journal* 2 (Spring 1958), 12.

_____. "The Orff Schulwerk in American Education," The Orff Echo 1, supplement no. 3 (May 1969).

Warner, Brigitte. "Creative Play-Acting with Children." The Orff Echo 1 (June 1969), 1.

Welsh, J. Robert. "Piano: Orff-Kodály." *Musart* 22, No. 5 (April–May 1970), 40–41.

Wilmouth, Jean Jr. "Let Children Move," *The Orff Echo* 2 (February 1970), 5.

Organizations

American Orff-Schulwerk Association. PO Box 391089, Cleveland, OH 44139